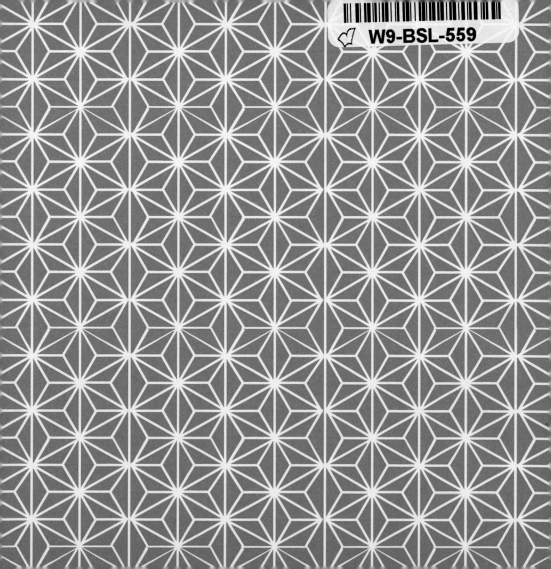

500

beers

500
beers

the only beer compendium you'll ever need

Zak Avery

SELLERS

PUBLISHING

A Quintet Book

Published by Sellers Publishing, Inc.
161 John Roberts Road, South Portland, Maine 04106
For ordering information:
(800) 625-3386 Toll Free
(207) 772-6814 Fax
Visit our Web site: www.sellerspublishing.com
E-mail: rsp@rsvp.com

ISBN: 978-1-4162-0788-7
Library of Congress Control Number: 2009931644
QTT.FBE

This book was conceived, designed, and produced by
Quintet Publishing Limited
6 Blundell Street
London N7 9BH
United Kingdom

Series Editor: Robert Davies
Assistant Editor: Carly Beckerman
Photography: Martin Norris
Designers: Rod Teasdale, Zoe White
Art Director: Michael Charles
Managing Editor: Donna Gregory
Publisher: James Tavendale

10 9 8 7 6 5 4 3 2 1

Printed in China by 1010 Printing International Ltd.

contents

introduction	6
glossary	12
water, malt, hops & yeast	20
selecting, storing & serving	42
lager—the global giant	60
english ale, british beer	100
wheat beer	140
wild & fruity	148
famous belgians	166
IPA	178
trappist & abbey beer	196
barley wine & old ale	220
porter & stout	232
oddities, rarities & specialties	258
index & credits	280

introduction

The world of beer is full of weird and wonderful brews. I've been drinking them for about twenty-five years now, and I've come to realize that simply by paying attention to what is in my beer glass, and trying to vary it as much as possible, I've gained a greater understanding and enjoyment of that apparently simple drink—beer. It's a humble, everyday beverage that is easily taken for granted, but it has a long pedigree.

Beer is one of the world's oldest manufactured drinks. It seems likely that beer was brewed as long ago as 6000 BCE in Sumeria and Babylonia. Unsurprisingly, brewing techniques were very different then—a cereal porridge may have been left in the sun and slowly fermented by accident—although it is worth noting that there is a recipe (of sorts) found in Egyptian tombs dating from around 2500 BCE. So it's true that beer is as old as civilization. In fact, without the process of sterilizing dirty water by boiling it to make beer, civilization might have perished by now.

This book is a celebration of that civilizing influence, of its variety of flavor, aroma, and color. True to the title, there are 500 beers presented here, but they are not necessarily the 500 best, or rarest, or strongest. Sure, there are very strong, very rare, and (in my opinion) very good beers included, but there are also beers that have perhaps become such a part of the landscape as to become invisible—familiarity breeds contempt, after all. Many of these are worth revisiting with an open mind, and some are minor classics. This book isn't a trophy-hunter's guide to beer, but more of a cross-section of what's out there—a user's guide to the world of beer.

As you move through the chapters of this book, the beers tend to get stronger and more intensely flavored. Color and strength are two easy ways to give you an idea of how a beer will taste. By the time you get to the end of this book, you will be a beer expert of sorts. If you find a beer that you recognize, the beers in the same spread are (mostly) in the same style. They're not exactly the same, but I've tried to group similar beers together. It will help your education if, along the way, you find time to go out and try some of the beers listed here. Or if not these beers, something you've never tried before. That's the sort of homework we should all enjoy, so I hope you try to fit it in.

But I'm not advocating ticking off lots of different beers, or drinking only beers new to you—there is a lot of pleasure in finding a favorite that you return to time and time again. But what I do believe is that by varying what you drink, and paying attention to how it feels as it slides past the gums, you can gain a greater enjoyment of beer than you ever thought possible. It's not a money-back guarantee, but it might be the best offer you get this week. What have you got to lose? If, at the end of the journey, you decide that the variety and flavor on offer in the wide world of beer isn't for you, well, at least you'll have had some fun along the way. At best, you might realize that the variety and quality out there is something worth celebrating. What's the worst that can happen?

Care to join me for one?

how to use this book

Beers are grouped according to the style. Broadly speaking, the book is organized so that the styles of beer get progressively darker and more intense.

pilsner

Pilsner is the classic expression of the golden, sparkling lager that we know today. The beers shown here are great representatives of that style, based as they are on the first golden lagers brewed in the Czech town of Plze (Pilsen, hence "pilsner"). They are mostly light-bodied but have a soft, malty roundness to them, followed by a dry and gently bitter hop finish. Dry, hoppy pilsners are great aperitif beers and can be good all-rounders for many foods. And let's not forget that you can also just drink them; served cold from a fridge on a hot day, nothing else quite hits the spot.

The classic beer in each style comes with quick food pairing ideas for the perfect culinary experience.

Picturesque Pilsner Urquell Brewery in the Czech Republic

Flag icons indicate which country each beer comes from.

Jever Pilsener

The strongly grassy aroma of this very pale pilsner reminds some of cats, or even skunks. It's true that this is a well-hopped lager, with only a passing impression of pale malt on the palate before the drying hop bitterness of the finish kicks in. Enjoyably austere.

Food match: robust snack food—ham, salami, or fried or tempura shrimp with a squeeze of lemon
Country: Germany
ABV: 4.9%; Serving temp.: 48–50°

LIGHT | DARK
LIGHT-BODIED | FULL-BODIED

AB-Inbev Staropramen

Pouring a lovely burnished gold color, Staropramen has an appetizing aroma—pale malt, a yeasty spiciness, and a hint of citrus pith (grapefruit?) in the mix. In the mouth, a textbook example of a pilsner—sweet pale malt followed by a gently bitter Saaz hop kick. Great balance.
Country: Czech Republic
ABV: 5%; Serving temp.: 48–50°

LIGHT | DARK
LIGHT-BODIED | FULL-BODIED

Schönram Pils

A very pale golden pilsner, with a nice grainy pale malt aroma and a spicy hop note. In the mouth, the hop character is much more pronounced, although still balanced. The hops come to the fore even more in the drying finish, with a long, persistent bitterness.
Country: Germany
ABV: 5%; Serving temp.: 48–55°

LIGHT | DARK
LIGHT-BODIED | FULL-BODIED

Zatecky Pivovar Zatec

There's a good depth of flavor and a surprising amount going on in this golden pilsner. Although the aroma doesn't give much away, the palate has a nice grainy sweetness, while the finish slides elegantly from malty sweetness to a faintly phenolic, bitter dryness.
Country: Czech Republic
ABV: 4.6%; Serving temp.: 48–50°

LIGHT | DARK
LIGHT-BODIED | FULL-BODIED

Dinkelacker-Schwaben Meister Pils

The Tettnang hops used in this beer are detectable as a spicy note in the aroma, and after a little sweetness mid-palate, appear as a dry, grassy note in the enjoyably bitter finish.
Country: Germany
ABV: 4.9%; Serving temp.: 44–48°

LIGHT | DARK
LIGHT-BODIED | FULL-BODIED

lager—the global giant   63

The temperature at which you serve beer can dramatically affect your drinking experience. Follow our basic guidelines to gain maximum flavor from your drink.

These scales show the color and the intensity of the beer.

This number shows the percentage of alcohol by volume.

glossary

%abv
percentage alcohol by volume—the proportionate amount of alcohol in any liquid. For beer, usually between 4% and 6%, although can be much higher.

adjunct
any source of *fermentable sugar* that isn't malted barley. Includes ingredientss uch as malted or unmalted wheat, rye and oats, corn, maize, and even raw sugar.

ale
a clear beer brewed with *top-fermenting yeast*, usually with a relatively short *fermentation* and maturation time. Ales should be served at around 55ºF to allow the fruity flavors to be best appreciated.

aroma hops
hops added late in the brewing process, which contribute primarily to the aroma rather than the bitterness of the beer.

attack
the initial impression that a beer makes as it hits the tongue.

barley
the grain upon which beer is built. The seed of the barley plant is *germinated* and *kilned* to make *malt*.

barrel-aging
the storage of beer in wooden barrels to allow *fermentation* to continue, while adding complexity from the *barrel flora* present.

barrel flora
the micro-organisms that live inside a wooden barrel, principally taken to mean lactobacillus and pediococcus bacteria and *brettanomyces* yeast, but in reality may contain many hundreds more.

bittering hops
hops added early in the brewing process, which contribute primarily to the bitterness rather than the aroma of the beer.

body
the impression of texture and flavor that a beer gives to the *palate*.

bottle-conditioning
yeast added at bottling that allows a beer to referment in the bottle to gain extra complexity.

bottom-fermenting yeast
a *yeast* that works at the bottom of a fermentation vessel, usually at lower temperatures, producing clean, crisp flavors.

brettanomyces
a strain of wild yeast noted for its ability to ferment most types of sugar and leave a characteristic aroma behind. See *funk*.

brew kettle
the vessel in which the *wort* is boiled, and to which the *hops* are added.

CAMRA
the UK-based Campaign for Real Ale, a consumer organization that promotes and celebrates *real ale*.

carbonation
the amount of dissolved carbon dioxide (CO_2) in a beer, which is released as fizz in the glass and on the tongue. Under- or over-carbonation can have a dramatic impact on how a beer is perceived.

cask ale

an *ale* that has refermented in the cask from which it is dispensed, and served without additional gas pressure.

cask-aging

allowing a beer a period of maturation in a barrel that has previously been used to store something else—usually whiskey, but might be sherry, wine, or anything else you care to imagine. NOTE: This has nothing to do with cask ale.

civet

a type of Indonesian cat, key to the production of Kopi Luwak coffee beans, which pass through its intestine before being harvested. (See entry for Mikkeller Beer Geek Breakfast Pooh Coffee Cask Festival Edition.)

condition

used to describe the quality of *cask ale*, based upon the development of flavor and amount of carbon dioxide dissolved in the beer.

copper

brewer's term for the *brew kettle*.

craft brewing

brewing beer with a focus on flavor and quality. The antonym of *macro*.

drinkability

the overall combination of flavor and *mouthfeel* that makes a beer interesting and enjoyable to drink.

ester

an aroma compound released during *fermentation*.

extreme beer

beer brewed with unconventional ingredients, of unusual intensity, with unusually high levels of alcohol. Predominantly an American obsession.

fermentation

the process whereby *yeast* converts sugar to alcohol. The yeast ingests the *fermentable sugars* and excretes alcohol, carbon dioxide, and *esters*.

fermentable sugar

the sugar released from the *malt* during the *mash*, then held in suspension in the *wort*.

finish

the impression that a beer leaves after it has been swallowed. Alternatively, the quality imparted to a beer that has been *cask-aged*.

funk, funky

the characteristic result of *brettanomyces* yeast fermentation—an unusual and not always pleasant aroma that, in small amounts, can add welcome complexity to a beer.

GABF

the Great American Beer Festival, held every year in Denver and still growing in popularity. There is a story attributed to the late beer writer Michael Jackson, who in the early 1980s brought an American brewer to the *GBBF*. The visiting brewer was so impressed that he said, "We've got to do this in America." "What would you use for beer?" was Michael's pithy response.

GBBF

the Great British Beer Festival. An annual celebration of *cask ale*, held in London, attended by as wide a variety of people as you are ever likely to see in one place, united in their love of great beer.

germinating

the process of sprouting a grain (usually *barley*) to release enzymes and fermentable sugars. The seed thinks it is going to grow into a plant, but the *maltster* has other plans for it.

grist

malt that has been processed through a mill, cracking the hard outer husk and releasing the powdery sugars and enzymes within.

hangover

the result of overindulging in any alcoholic drink. May vary in severity from a slight sluggishness to a full-blown existential crisis. Moderation is the key to avoidance.

haze, hazy

very fine proteins in suspension in a beer. If a beer is unfiltered, these proteins become visible at lower temperatures. Harmless, but a good indication that your *ale* is being served too cold.

hop

the flower of the hop plant *Humulus lupulus*, which is used to impart bitterness, flavor, and aroma to beer. Venerated like a god in some parts of North America.

hop back

the large strainer vessel that is used to remove spent *hops* from the boiled *wort*.

keg beer

a stable, filtered (and sometimes, but not always, pasteurized) beer that is dispensed from its metal barrel via additional gas pressure. Once reviled, there is now a quiet resurgence in quality keg beer.

kilning

the process of cooking the *germinated barley* to arrest further growth. Can also be used as a way of coloring and flavoring the grain.

lauter

the process of recirculating *wort* out of the bottom of the *mash tun* and back into the top. Lautering is done to help clarify the *wort*.

liquor

brewer's term for water.

lager

a beer brewed with *bottom-fermenting yeast*, usually with a relatively long *fermentation* and maturation time. Lagers should be served at around 40°F to accentuate their crispness.

macro

usually used to mean any mass-produced adjunct lager. The antithesis of *craft brewing*.

malt

usually made from *barley* (but can be made from any grain), a grain seed that has been *germinated* and *kilned*. When processed through a mill, it becomes *grist*.

maltster

the person charged with creating malt from grain. Employed by a maltings.

mash

the porridge-like mixture of hot *liquor* and *grist* that releases the *fermentable sugars* from the *malt*. Once the mash is *lautered* and clarified, it becomes *wort*.

mash tun

the vessel in which the *mash* takes place.

mouthfeel

the overall impression of the beer in the mouth; includes *attack, body, carbonation,* and *finish.*

nitrogenated

the use of nitrogen (and other gases) under pressure to produce a creamy body and head for a beer, most often seen in draft Guinness.

palate

of the mouth, the sensory organs that perceive taste and smell. Of a beer, the impression that is made upon those organs.

pasteurization

the process of flash-heating any foodstuff to kill any unwanted bacteria present. Unsurprisingly, this has a detrimental impact on the flavor of beer.

pitching

the act of adding *yeast* to the cooled *wort* to start *fermentation.*

pith

the white rind between the outer skin and inner flesh of a citrus fruit. Particularly bitter, it is often used to describe the character of hoppy beers.

real ale

any beer that has undergone an intentional secondary refermentation in the vessel from which it is dispensed. Includes *cask ale* and *bottle-conditioned* beer.

reinheitsgebot
the German purity law of 1516, which stipulated that beer could contain only water, malt, and hops.

session beer
any light-*bodied*, lower *abv* beer, usually (but not exclusively) *ales*. So-called because their lower strength allows you to have a few of them in one session.

sparge
after the *wort* is run from the *mash tun*, more hot water is sprayed on top of the spent grain to wash any residual *fermentable sugar* out of the grain. This technique is known as *sparging*.

spontaneous fermentation
fermentation that starts without the addition of a cultured *yeast*, initiated by *wild yeasts* in the atmosphere. A disaster, in most brewers' opinion, although celebrated by the lambic brewers of Belgium.

top-fermenting yeast
a *yeast* that works at the top of a fermentation vessel, usually at warmer temperatures, producing flowery, fruity, *estery* flavors.

water
the main ingredient by volume of beer. Historically, the relative hardness of water dictated the style of beer that was brewed. Now, water can be filtered and corrected to whatever style the brewer wishes.

wild yeast
uncultured *yeasts* that exist everywhere, which enjoy nothing more than ruining a batch of perfectly good beer with their unpredictable actions.

wort
the sweet liquid full of *fermentable sugar* that results from the combination of hot *liquor* and *grist*.

water, malt, hops & yeast

Looking at the ingredients list, you might think that beer isn't a complicated foodstuff, and in some ways, you'd be right. The four basic ingredients are water, malted barley, hops, and yeast—surely it can't be that fiddly? Well, as with all cooking, it's straightforward as long as you follow the recipe, but there are a surprising number of variables.

Water—how variable can that be? As it turns out, it's very variable, largely due to the geology of the location of the brewery. Water filters through rock, picking up mineral deposits on the way, and these minerals make their presence known in various ways. Just as washing your hands with soap feels different in hard and soft water areas (soap foams more easily in softer water), brewing with hard or soft water affects how the beer feels in the mouth.

Barley is a crop, and like all agricultural products, it can vary from year to year. However, the variation in harvest quality is small when compared to how radically the grain changes after the processing necessary to prepare it for brewing. It can come in as many shades as ordinary breakfast toast, from pale and barely cooked to blackened and burned.

Hops are an agricultural product that can vary hugely from year to year, not only in quality but also in quantity. At the time of writing, the brewing world is sighing with relief after a good harvest—the previous two years were disastrous in terms of quantity, if not quality. For something that contributes such a significant and robust flavor, hops are surprisingly delicate plant blossoms.

And yeast—well, as we shall see, yeast can make or ruin a beer, and surprisingly, a spoiled beer isn't always bad news....

water

It seems odd, but most beer is around 95% water. If a beer is 5% alcohol by volume (abv), then clearly the rest of the liquid is nothing but what goes into the brew kettle at the start of the process. Even if you allow a small amount of volume for the compounds that make beer look, smell, and taste the way it does (and there is a large range of color, aroma, and flavor across all the different styles of beer), then most of what you pay for is what comes out of the tap.

Although it's a bit disingenuous to suggest that beer is just processed tap water, the majority of breweries do use the local main water supply for making beer. This water will be filtered, stripped of all its component minerals, making it completely pure, and then have certain mineral salts put back in. There are a number of breweries that do use water from underground lakes, drawing from their own wells, but these are relatively unusual, and most of them correct the mineral content of their water. I'm afraid that the myth of beer brewed from untreated natural spring water is, in almost every case, just a myth.

That's not to say that water isn't an important element. There are certain styles of beer that are closely linked to the composition of the water where they originate. The rounded softness of classic Czech pilsners is related to the relatively low quantity of mineral salts in the water. The high sulfate content of hard Burton water emphasizes hop bitterness and dryness—qualities both prevalent in the classic pale ales of Burton. The soft water in London—the home of porter and stout brewing—is high in chlorides, which gives beer a fuller mouthfeel.

Clean water is essential to life, but it's only relatively recently that we have been lucky enough to have a constant potable supply. Before clean water was a fact of life, beer had the advantage of having been boiled during production, sterilizing it and killing any water-borne bacteria. Beer for breakfast was a way of life, rather than a fantasy. Admittedly it was a weak beer, brewed with partly used malt, and known as "small beer" (that's the origin of the term). While we're talking trivia, it's worth noting that brewers refer to water in the brewery as "liquor." I've asked a lot of brewers why this is, and the reply has always been "we just do."

Three of the basic ingredients of beer—water, barley, and hops

Water, despite being the main ingredient by volume in beer, is perhaps the least important. As long as it is clean and drinkable, it can be changed to suit the style of beer being brewed, or altered to a composition that corresponds with the brewery's "house style." The other ingredients, as we shall see, are rather more complex.

malt

Malt, or more strictly speaking, malted barley, will be something most of us have seen in its raw form, perhaps without realizing it, and often without making the connection to beer. Whenever you see fields of barley waving serenely in the summer breeze, you are looking at an important ingredient of beer. But quite a complicated process is involved to get the grain from the field to the glass, and many of the steps are crucial to the quality of the finished product. Also crucial to quality is the variety of barley. Every brewer has his own preferences, and the choice may be influenced by the style of beer that is being brewed. There are a couple of classic English varieties that are prized for their depth of flavor (if you see Maris Otter or Golden Promise listed as an ingredient, you're onto a good thing). Or rather, at least the brewer has bought the best grain; it's up to him to finish the job properly.

We'll leave out the harvesting process—there isn't a lot of romance in describing a field of barley being cut and processed by a vehicle the size of a house. It's impressive, sure, but what's important is to know that what is harvested is just the ears of grain at the very top of the plant. What is left at the end of the process is a big pile of grain—usually barley (but wheat, oats, and rye can also be used) complete with its tough outer husk. This is basically a seed—plant it, and more barley will grow. This basic natural process, a seed sprouting when it's planted, is what forms the next step of the production process.

Raw barley grains are as hard as little stones, but they contain the starch and enzymes that are needed to turn the body of the grain into fermentable sugar. Yeast needs this sugar to produce alcohol and carbon dioxide, but we'll come to yeast a little later. It is the specialized job of the maltster to oversee this process, from the germination of the malt through to cooking it, to stabilize and (sometimes) color it.

At the maltings, the grain is soaked with water, starting the process of germination and sprouting. If the little barleycorn was a sentient being, it would be thinking, "The rains have come! Now's my big chance to become a big strong barley plant." At this point, it releases enzymes that break down its reserves of starch into sugar that it thinks it will need to grow into a plant. A few days into this process, after lovingly turning and raking the grains to ensure that their sprouts don't get too tangled, and that the grains have enough air to stop them from going moldy, the maltster plays his cruelest trick. Rather than allowing the grains to carry on their natural process of growth, he scoops them up, tosses them into a hot rotating oven, and cooks them until they are effectively nothing more than little nuggets of fermentable sugar. Perhaps it's better that the little barleycorn isn't a sentient being after all—I wouldn't like to imagine its thoughts at this ignominious end. Happily, the little barleycorn hasn't died in vain. He's been converted into pale malt, which is the basic ingredient for most beers.

Over 130 million tons of barley are grown around the world each year

Malt heaped on the malting floor of Austria's Freistädter Brewery

This isn't quite the end of the story. In the roasting process, the maltster has the option to continue cooking the malt beyond its pale stage, at a higher temperature, so that it starts to color, exactly as bread does when it is toasted. A little more time, and the malt picks up a browner hue, with a nuttier taste. More still, and it becomes dark brown, tasting of coffee and bitter chocolate. Sometimes, the barley is left slightly damp before the kilning process, and so the sugar in the grain caramelizes slightly as it dries, producing toffeeish grain with a red-brown color—Vienna malt, used to produce Vienna-style lagers.

There is also the option of using something other than a neutral heat source to cook the grain. It's a much more unusual, artisanal process to kiln malt over a natural heat source, usually peat or wood. With this heat, there is, of course, smoke; malt dried in this way takes on a deep, smoky aroma that is passed on to the finished beer. Although unusual, these smoked malts are still used in beer production, most notably the smoked beers ("Rauchbiere," in their native tongue) of Franconia in central Germany. They are also sometimes used in small quantities to fill out and add complexity to stouts and porters.

Each of these malts has its own character that influences how the finished beer will turn out. Looking at the color of a stout, you might think that it is brewed only from very heavily roasted malt, but surprisingly the malt bill (as the combination of malts in any given brew is known) is predominantly pale malt—perhaps around 70%, with the rest being darker roast malt (and perhaps some dark roasted unmalted barley). The key thing to remember is that pale malt is used for fermentable sugar and without a large proportion of it, you're not going to get beer at the end, but unfermented barley tea. I've never tried this, but my hunch is that it isn't as interesting as beer.

One final thing happens to malt before it is ready for brewing. The grains are passed through a mill—a pair of heavy steel rollers with a very small gap between them. This cracks the hard outer husk of the grain and releases the floury starch inside. Some breweries choose to do this themselves, but it is often done at the maltings. The grist (as the combination of husk and center is known) is what is mixed with water in the brew kettle. That's part of the brewing process, which we'll come to in a little while, but not before we talk about the two other important ingredients in brewing—hops and yeast.

hops

There's a cruel trick I like to play whenever I hold a beer tasting. I get a tulip glass of beer, swirl it around, hold it under someone's nose, and ask what they smell. For most people, it's very hard to pick out more than one or two aromas in a beer, and harder still to put a name to them. The most common word that people say when put under the spotlight is "hoppy?" The question mark is very important—everyone knows that beer has hops in and that most beers taste and smell hoppy to some degree. But what does a hop really smell like? And now you come to mention, what actually is a hop?

The answer to the first question is that hops smell like lots of things, and they also only smell like hops. The element that smells like hops is a bit pungent, a bit musty, and somehow almost a bit dirty—this is an underlying hop quality that is common to all hops. The element that smells like lots of different things differs according to the hop variety. Hops can smell of lemon, grapefruit, pine needles, black currant, jasmine—you can see why people look hopeful when they stab at hops being what they can smell. On the plus side, of course, they are usually right.

To answer the second question, hops are the flower of the climbing plant *Humulus lupulus*. As a farmed plant, they grow up wires and poles, and in the wild, they climb anything that gets in their way. And how they climb—they can easily grow from tiny shoots up to twenty feet tall in a season, and are harvested in late summer. Fresh hops are an intense olfactory experience—they are sticky with their natural resins, almost overpoweringly pungent, and smell unlike anything else. The dominant aroma at this stage is usually a resinous, pine sap-like note. When hops are dried, and then boiled in beer (or rubbed in the palm of the hand), their secondary character comes out—the notes of citrus, blossom, and fruit that were mentioned earlier. When used in beer, they principally add bitterness and aroma, dependent on what point they are added in the brewing process. They also have an antibacterial quality that once helped preserve beer; in times past, this used to be a great help at keeping beer free from bacterial infection, but it is less of an issue in the hygienic world of twenty-first-century brewing.

The biggest hop-producing area in the world is Germany's Hallertau Valley

Oast houses are traditional English farm buildings used for drying
hops in preparation for the brewing process

There used to be something of a schism about hops in the world of brewing. There were the four classic European varieties (Saaz, Tettnang, Spalt, and Hallertau, the so-called noble hops), understated British varieties (East Kent Golding, Fuggles, and the like), and exuberantly pungent American hops (Cascade, Chinook, et al.). Each was viewed with suspicion by the others, and never the twain shall meet. Happily, those days of hop apartheid are over, and brewers all over the world merrily use hops from wherever best suits the style of beer that they want to make. I've had outstanding British bitter in St. Louis, Missouri, resinous American-style pale ale in Cornwall, and the best tasting pilsner ever from a brewery in northern Italy.

Hops are the spice of beer. They add zest and excitement to the stolid, sweet backbone that the malt provides. They are the chutney in a cheese sandwich, the jalapeños on a pile of cheesy nachos. The interplay between hops and malt is what makes beer interesting—in fact, it's what makes beer beer. But there is one further ingredient that adds its own unique influence, that magically transmutes sugar into alcohol—yeast.

yeast

OK, so it's a bit of a reach to suggest that yeast does its job magically. It's actually a simple biological process whereby the yeast eats the sugar and excretes carbon dioxide (CO_2), alcohol, and esters (aroma compounds), the process known as fermentation. But even if they are not magical little creatures, yeasts are pretty incredible.

Yeasts are single-celled organisms, and they are all around us—floating in the air, sitting on the skins of fruit, hanging around between your toes, waiting for something to do. There are lots of different types of yeast, but as far as brewing goes, there are only three types that matter—*Saccharomyces cerevisae* (ale yeast), *S. uvarum* (lager yeast), and wild yeast (principally *Brettanomyces bruxellensis*). Of these two, *S. cerevisae* and *S. uvarum* are cultivated, cultured yeasts, whereas *B. bruxellensis* is a sort of rogue yeast that floats around looking for something nice to spoil. It's the two yeasts of the genus *Saccharomyces* that are the important ones, but we'll talk a bit about naughty old *Brett* in a while too.

Both ale and lager yeasts do pretty much the same thing—they eat sugar, and leave behind carbon dioxide, alcohol, and flavor compounds. But it's the way they do it that makes the difference. Lager yeasts like to ferment at lower temperatures, lounging around at the bottom of the fermenting vessel, and they tend toward longer, slower fermentations. This process produces much cleaner, crisper-tasting beers. This long, slow fermentation, referred to as lagering (from the German "lagern," meaning "to store"), is how the classic golden beer got its name.

Ale yeast likes to get itself all worked up into a lather at the top of the fermenting vessel, producing big pillowing heads of foam, working at warmer temperatures and fermenting much faster. This style of fermentation produces much fruitier, more complex flavors. This is the principal difference between lagers and ales; even in beers made only with pale malt, the difference that the yeast makes is profound.

There are, of course, exceptions to the rule. One interesting hybrid still in production today, Anchor Steam beer, is an example of the style known as California Common. This is a beer fermented with a lager yeast, but

Ale yeast rises to the top of the beer during fermentation

at warmer temperatures. It predates the widespread affordability of refrigeration and produces a medium-bodied beer with the fruity attributes of an ale. It's not a lagerbier, as it doesn't have the long period of cold fermentation (sometimes referred to as cold conditioning) that a true lager has. Other exceptions are the German regional specialties kölsch and altbier. These are beers fermented with an ale yeast, but which receive a period of cold conditioning. They are lagerbiers, and yet are neither ales nor lagers. You see how complex yeast is?

Talking of complex, wild yeasts take this to another level. I singled out *Brettanomyces* earlier, as it's a relatively well-known wild yeast, notable for leaving rather unpleasant barnyard aromas behind after completing its work. I'm being a little unfair, because this is just one of many wild yeasts that work their magic in the spontaneously fermenting lambic beers of Belgium. Lambic is a style that challenges the very definition of what beer is, producing as it does tart, dry, acidic beers that need many months and years of aging and blending before they are drinkable. It's also unfair to point the finger solely at yeasts, as there are a host of micro-organisms that live in the wooden maturation barrels and give the beer a hard time.

But all this talk of wild yeasts isn't making anything simpler, and neither is the fact that both ale and lager yeasts have many hundreds of different strains to them, each subtly affecting the final taste of the beer. One brewery may use its own house strain, another might be happy to buy a known cultured strain of yeast from a yeast bank. The key is that the brewer has to provide conditions in which the yeast will thrive and do what it's meant to do, in a predictable manner. There is a joke that a brewer's job is just to keep the yeast happy—happy yeasts make good beer. And with that uplifting thought in our minds, let's turn to how beer is made.

It wasn't until the mid-nineteenth century that the role played by fresh yeast in beermaking was properly understood

Yeast forms a smooth creamy cap in a traditional open fermenter

brewing

Water, malt, hops, and yeast—just four ingredients. How hard can brewing be? Well, the answer is that brewing itself is actually a pretty straightforward process; the trick is correctly manipulating all the variables to get the desired effect. When you add in all the different types of water that can be added, the many shades and quantities of malt that can be used, the combination of hops, and the choice of yeast strains that all do slightly different things, you can see that pretty quickly the choices mount up to a dazzling number of outcomes. No wonder that every beer tastes different and we all have our favorites.

The first step is to create a sort of coarse porridge from the grain and the hot water. This is called the mash, and its purpose is to release the fermentable sugar from the cracked grain, or grist. The vessel in which it is done is called the mash tun. The mash slts at around 150°F for about an hour to allow the enzymes in the malt to get to work and release all the fermentable sugar from the grist. This sweet liquid is called wort (pronounced "wurt").

Once all the fermentable sugar has been extracted, the wort needs to be clarified. This is done by a process known as lautering—recirculating the wort out of the bottom of the mash tun, and spraying it back on the top of the mashed grain (the spraying is known as sparging—brewers love to have a special term for everything). In the lautering process, the mashed grain, which is now basically a floating plug of grain husks, acts as a filter. The wort goes into the top, filters down through the spent grain, and comes out clear at the bottom. This second pass also ensures that all of the sugar is extracted from the mash.

That's the fiddly bit over with. Then comes the boil, where it starts to feel like brewing as you might imagine it. The wort is heated to boiling point in a new vessel (it will boil for about an hour), and the hop additions start. There are certain varieties of hops that are better suited to being added early (after about ten minutes). These early additions are known as bittering hops, as they contribute the background bitterness of the beer. The later in the boil you add hops, the more they contribute to the aroma rather than the bitterness. Certain hop varieties are more suited to being added later in the boil, and these are called (yes, you've guessed it)

Brewing kettle in Feierling Brewery, Freiburg, Germany

aroma hops. At the end of the boil, you can try the wort (careful, it's hot). It will be pretty sweet, as there is all that sugar the yeast is dying to get to work on, but it should be starting to taste a bit like beer.

The end of the boil is also the point where things have to move a bit more quickly. You remember what I said about wild yeasts being all around us? Well, it's not quite an emergency, but from the end of the boil, everything that comes into contact with the wort needs to be sterile. The faster you remove the hops and cool the wort, the sooner you can add the yeast and get the fermenting vessel airtight (with one-way airlock), keeping out all those naughty wild yeasts that want to ruin your beer. Once the wort is cooled to around 75°F, the yeast can be added (or pitched, as the experts like to say). Fermentation begins quickly after pitching.

Primary fermentation is a surprisingly vigorous process—it will throw up a big head of foam. After a couple of days, this will die back, and a slower second fermentation begins, which might last as long as four weeks (or more with a stronger beer). At the end of the primary fermentation, there will be a lot of dead yeast (known as trub) and goodness knows what else at the bottom of the fermenter. It's usually a good idea to move the beer (yes, it's beer by this point) into a clean vessel to complete its fermentation, as the trub can cause unpleasant flavors and odors to form. A couple more weeks of gentle fermentation, and it's ready to be bottled or kegged, and drunk a few weeks after that.

This isn't a complete "how to" guide for brewing—I've left out a lot of details for simplicity's sake—but that's basically how you brew beer. Four ingredients, some cooking, and a long wait—that's all there is to it. From that basic process, the whole world of beer is created.

brewery tours & visits

The English phrase "he couldn't organize a piss-up in a brewery" is often used to describe incompetence. Happily, I've never known this literally to be the case. It might not surprise you too much to hear that visiting a brewery should be an interesting and enjoyable way to pass a few hours. It might not always end in a party, but what you do come away with is a sense of what makes one brewery different from another, and why beers vary between breweries, within a brewery's output, and indeed, sometimes from batch to batch.

Having toured many breweries, I'm always amazed at the enormous number of variables that are available to a brewer. Multiply the number of malt styles by the number of hop varieties by the number of yeast strains, and you have a very large number indeed—and that's before you start to combine malts and hops in different proportions. Given this, you would imagine a brewer to be a cross between a philosopher and a mad scientist, but the range of people you're likely to meet standing over a steaming copper is as broad as anywhere. Each will have his own way of doing things, their own little twist to the brewing process, and that is what makes a brewery visit worthwhile—you'll get an insight that you will never get from just drinking their products, and this insight will enrich your enjoyment of their beer.

Most breweries are surprisingly happy to show people around, although it's rare for them to drop everything to show one person the brewery. It might help to get a group together and call yourselves a local beer appreciation society. At one end of the scale, you might get a private tour of the brewery, with a tasting thrown in. If this happens, make sure that you are gracious enough to buy some beer at the end of it—they aren't just giving up their time for fun, you know. At the other extreme, you might be told to join the monthly tour, or (a very few cases) just get a flat "No." Don't take it personally—although the end product is usually enjoyed in a sociable setting, it is born of hard work, and the work needs to come first. Actually, in the course of compiling this book, I had a few breweries tell me they were too busy to send me beer. That, of course, is another thing altogether...

Larger breweries often display a selection of old and outdated brewing equipment

selecting, storing & serving

As with any artisan product, it can feel a bit intimidating if you are on the outside with nothing but curiosity as your guide. Although beer is all around us, it is something that many people don't pay any attention to—it's just something cold and wet with which to blow away the dust of a hard day at work, or an excuse to spend time with friends in a pub or bar. Worse still, it can seem that there is an impenetrable language and etiquette associated with it.

While it's true that you have to pay a little more attention to fully appreciate good beer (and the majority of beers featured later in this book are worthy of appreciation), there aren't really as many rules as you might think. You don't need to over-analyze a beer to enjoy it—you are already equipped to tell the difference between a lager and a stout, by sight, smell, and taste. And if you think about those smells and tastes, you'll start to have an idea of which would be a better refreshing drink or appetizer (it's the lager, by the way). What you might not guess is that stout is great to serve with dessert, particularly if it includes chocolate or vanilla flavors.

However, there are a few rules of thumb that will help you to get the best from your beers, and these are set out in the next few pages. There are also a few tips on how to take beer appreciation beyond the kitchen or the bar, and into breweries and specialty stores. There is a world of flavor out there, so let's start with one of the basics—finding the good stuff.

Drinking beer outside on a summer evening, a cool pale beer might be a good choice

selecting beer

Forget champagne, cocktails, and after-dinner liqueurs—there really is a beer for every occasion. As I sit here writing this, late at night, I'm enjoying a nightcap of Moorhouse's Black Cat. It's a dark beer, which I always associate with evening drinking. It's fairly low in alcohol (3.4%abv) because I have to get up early in the morning, and also because I need to focus on the job in hand. It has a creamy chocolatey edge to it that's a little bit like a bedtime cup of cocoa. It's not so full of flavor that it is distracting me from my work, but it has just enough to keep my attention. It's cellar-cool, but not cold, because that would take the edge off the delicate flavors. If I didn't have to write, or get up early, I might have gone for something a little stronger, but on this occasion, this beer fits the bill.

Of course, there are times when I want something a bit more spritzy. A cold pilsner is a great way of rousing the appetite—Jever Pilsener, for example, with its rasping, dry bitterness, or (if I have someone to share a bottle with) a very cold Duvel. Depending on what's for dinner, Victory Hop Devil IPA or Schneider Weisse wheat beer might be good. If we're pushing the boat out and having dessert, Sam Smith's Imperial Stout or Liefman's Kriek will fit the bill (particularly with anything based on chocolate). Anyone for cheese? Gosh, we're making an evening of it now; better break out the barley wine or old ale—Anchor Old Foghorn or, if I'm feeling extravagant, a twelve-year-old bottle of Thomas Hardy Ale.

That's focusing on beer with food. Sometimes, you just want to drink a beer. It's very important not to lose sight of that—beer is made for drinking. It's essentially a simple pleasure, and although there are some people who insist on drinking only the rarest, strongest, most challenging beers, it doesn't have to be that way. There is no inclusivity in that point of view. I believe that beer appreciation doesn't begin and end with drinking the rarest, strongest, wildest beers imaginable. That's actually beer snobbery. As someone who enjoys beer in all of its forms, I know that there is some pleasure to be found in almost any brew, even if that pleasure is solely to slake a thirst or rouse an appetite. Don't listen to the snobs and purists—it's your beer, and you can enjoy it however you want. There aren't really any rights or wrongs when it comes to beer. It's mostly common sense, dictated by how you feel. If you want refreshing, pick something light in color and lower in alcohol.

For something more profound, darker and stronger is the key. In fact, the color and strength of a beer can tell you a lot about how it will taste. The color might range from very pale gold to almost completely black, taking a journey from light, grainy character through to dark, roasted flavors. If you look at the strength, that will give you an idea of the intensity of the flavor—there are some very pale beers that tip the scales at around 9%abv, but you wouldn't drink them for refreshment. Not only is the flavor too intense to be truly refreshing, but that amount of alcohol needs to be sipped slowly and treated with respect. That's why there is a "color and intensity" graphic included for every beer in this book—think of it as an at-a-glance indicator of what you'll be getting. Of course, it won't give you the detail that the tasting note does, but it's useful to have this information presented graphically for all of the beers presented here, as a standard for comparison.

buying beer

As with any specialty product, there is a certain craft to tracking down and buying interesting and flavorful beers. As modern life seems to speed up and miniaturize, this paradoxically seems to put more pressure on our time, not less. Buying beer is something that is done with the weekly grocery shop, and given that the range of beers available on the supermarket shelf has expanded in recent years, this isn't too bad an option any more. However, there will almost certainly be a specialty beer retailer near you, although they may be hidden away on a backstreet, or tucked away on an anonymous trading estate. Tracking them down can be an art in itself, and the best ones are usually word-of-mouth operations. Go to the best beer bar in town, ask a local wine retailer (he'll know—the drinks industry is very tight-knit), or get on the Internet and visit some of the Web sites mentioned in the "Further Reading" section.

If this seems like a lot of effort, you're right—it is. But I can guarantee that the range, the service, and the overall experience will be infinitely more agreeable than buying beer in a supermarket. It wasn't so long ago that every small town had specialty stores. These are now rarer sights due to the incursion of everything-under-one-roof supermarkets. Not only has the physical store gone, but gone with it is the expertise and passion that used to accompany it. It would be a shame to allow the same to happen to good beer retailers.

Specialty beer retailers can advise you and hand-pick beers to your taste

Specialty beer retailers offer a bewildering choice of brands

storing beer

There are very few beers that truly get better with age. The majority of bottled beers are designed to be drunk young; pale beers will start to degrade fairly soon after bottling, and hop character is also surprisingly fragile. Even beers that have a very assertive hop character will lose their edge after only a few months in the bottle. They won't be bad by any means, but mostly, the fresher the better. There are, of course, a few exceptions.

Bottle-conditioned beer is beer that has had a small dose of fresh yeast and sugar added at bottling. The purpose of this is to get the beer to referment in the bottle, which adds extra flavor and complexity. This beer is said to be "live"—it is "real ale," to use the term favored by the UK-based Campaign for Real Ale (CAMRA). These beers, dependent on their strength, will improve while in the bottle, although there are two important caveats here. The first is that beer of moderate strength won't improve indefinitely. There are some strong beers (over 9%abv) that can age and get better for a few years, but the majority of these bottle-conditioned beers are best within a year of bottling. The second important thing to remember is that bottle-conditioning can make a good beer great, but it can't make a bad beer good. In fact, if not done with great care, it can ruin perfectly good beer. To assume that bottle-conditioned beer is the best on the market is to miss out on lots of fabulous beer that has simply been micro-filtered and bottled.

serving beer

There are very few rules when it comes to serving beer, but one of the main ones is temperature. As a rule of thumb, the serving temperature should be close to the temperature of the secondary fermentation. Put simply, lagers should be around 40°F and ales should be around 55°F. If you like your ale colder, go ahead, but you'll be missing out on a lot of delicate aromas. If you prefer your lager served warmer, well, there's really not much hope for you—go back to the beginning of the book and start again.

It's worth knowing that the shape of the glass you drink from will drastically affect the aroma of the beer, and also the flavor (because smell and taste are very closely linked). Nobody ever believes this when I tell them, so go and get a beer, some different-shaped glasses (or coffee mugs or teacups), and see for yourself. You'll be amazed. For this reason, I like to stick to one shape of glass, as it removes a variable from how you perceive the beer. I like to use oversized wine glasses, which seems to infuriate beer purists, as they think I'm trying to get all fancy about beer. I'm not, I just like how a big wine glass displays aromas, and you can swirl beer around to release the aroma without it sloshing over the sides.

There is a very simple way to evaluate a beer—drink it! On one level, if you enjoy it, then it's a good beer. If you want to get a bit more involved, then use some more of your senses. Pour the beer into a glass and hold it up to the light. What color is it? This will give a big clue as to how it will taste. Is it clear, hazy, or cloudy? Is it meant to be? Give the beer a swirl and stick your nose in—what do you think? Does it smell good to you, or is there something amiss? Either way, you're going to have to drink some to get the full picture. As it hits the tongue, concentrate on how it feels—is it over-carbonated or flat? Is it overly sticky or dry? What about the texture or mouthfeel? What happens after you swallow? How do the flavors change, and how long do they last? Do it all again, and really swill it around your mouth, or suck some air in through it. Do you want another mouthful? Another bottle? A whole case (perhaps not in one sitting)?

I'm often asked how I got to be a beer expert, and what it's like to have the best job in the world. My standard reply to the second question is that it's the best job in the world apart from the hours and the money. To the first question, well, the only way to learn about beer is to drink it. I don't mean that you should drink lots of your favorite beer, but you should drink widely. Try new beers all the time. Try beers that you wouldn't normally imagine drinking. If you see a beer that you've never seen before, try it. Drink really bad, cheap beer, and spend what seems like a foolish amount of money on something rare and unusual. You have a palate, and you can train it, but only by exercising it. If you do this, I guarantee that the time (and money) you invest in doing this will repay you many times over. You will build an appreciation of one of the simplest pleasures in life—a glass of beer—and that appreciation will enrich every beer you drink.

Lager should ideally be kept chilled right until you're ready to drink it

It's normally considered acceptable for up to 5% of a glass of beer to be foam rather than liquid

tasting beer

There is a difference between drinking beer and formally tasting it, but that difference isn't huge. While it would be nice to think that everyone always devoted their full attention to every mouthful of beer, we know that reality isn't like that. I always try to give my full attention to the first few mouthfuls of beer, if only to make sure that it is everything it should be, and that it is free from flaws.

If you want to get really fancy about tasting beer, there are a few things you should bear in mind. As mentioned above, the shape of the glass makes a big difference to how you perceive the beer, so try to stick to the same-shaped glass each time you taste. My preference is for oversized wine glasses, but any tulip-shaped glass is good. The glass should be scrupulously clean—dishwasher-clean isn't really good enough, as the residues on the glass will at least spoil the head on the beer, and at worst will interfere with the aroma and flavor of the beer itself. Wash the glasses with a sponge and a little detergent, then rinse them very thoroughly under running water and polish them dry with a clean cloth.

Tasting itself should happen indoors—although drinking beer al fresco is a pleasure, it isn't really conducive to showing beers at their best. Pick a space that is brightly lit, preferably with natural light, and free from intrusive odors (even from these few points, you can already see that you can't really *taste* beer at a barbecue, you can only *drink* beer—no bad thing, I'm sure you'll agree). Pour out a small measure into your chosen tasting glass, and hold it up to the light. Look at the color, clarity, and intensity. Compare the very edge of the beer to the core color—the color at the center of the glass. While you're holding it up and eyeballing it, give it a little swirl and see how it reacts, and how the bubbles behave just below the surface—you're looking for a moderate carbonation. Carbonation, and how the beer behaves as it hits the tongue, is a hugely important factor in your perception of a beer, and yet is the least talked about.

But before the beer hits your tongue, give it one more gentle swirl and smell it. Get your nose into the mouth of the glass, and take a couple of shallow sniffs. You might find that you can detect more aroma if you keep your mouth slightly open, and take in some air through your mouth and nose at the same time. There will be a lot going on in the aroma, and picking out and putting names to the different scents is difficult, but it's something that can be learned.

The same is true of flavor. There are a surprising number of flavors in a beer, detectable in three phases—as the beer enters the mouth (the attack), as it crosses the palate (mid-palate), and after it has been swallowed (the aftertaste, or finish). Sweetness is usually perceived first, as the tongue has a greater concentration of sweet-sensing tastebuds at the front, while bitterness is perceived at the back of the tongue. After you swallow, there is another big burst of flavor and aroma, which may change as it lingers on the palate. These sensations arrive in a rush, and can be difficult to pick apart, but again, practice makes perfect.

You might decide to make some notes on your impressions. I find this useful, if only because what seems like a striking and distinctive beer at the moment of tasting will be a vague memory in a few days' time. It doesn't have to be an essay about the beer, but a few words to record the %abv, color, aroma, flavor, and finish can be a great aid to recalling the beer. If you really start to enjoy the process, there are plenty of beer-centric Web sites on which to record your thoughts (see "Further Reading").

A plea for common sense though. It's hard not to be impressed and swept away by big-bodied, strong beers, brewed with armfuls of hops and sackloads of malt. They don't lack balance, but some of them are just a bit overstuffed. They are the haute couture of the beer world—very impressive on the catwalk, but slightly absurd when you try to integrate them into everyday life. It's important to remember that the biggest beers aren't necessarily the best—sure, they're a lot of fun, but personally, the beers I like best are the ones I return to time and time again, and they aren't exclusively the rarities and the hop bombs. Beer appreciation is like beer itself—it's all about balance and moderation.

Exposing a beer to natural light is the only way to gauge color accurately

Beer can be matched to any food you enjoy, just like wine. Throughout the book we suggest some unconventional (but delicious) pairings.

beer & food

Beer and food matching is quite a hot topic at the moment. Although I enjoy it, I can't pretend to be an expert, and there are many books written on the subject that offer more insight than will be offered here. But there are some simple rules that can help show a beer (and the food too) at its best. The three rules are cut, complement, and contrast.

The cut is serving a beer that basically resets the palate with each sip. Some styles of food are suited to this—spicy, fatty foods work particularly well with strong IPAs, for example. The carbonation lifts the fat from the tongue, and the hops sweep in and scrub it clean, leaving it fresh for another mouthful.

The complement is a tricky one to pull off. It works by matching a flavor in the beer to a flavor in the dish. For example, German weissebier works very well with creamy curries. There is a similarity in the texture and flavor, but not such that each is emulating the other. It's a delicate balance that can be disastrous if the beer and food are too similar. In fact, as unlikely as it sounds, the more similar the flavors, the worse the match.

The contrast is my favorite technique. Rich, creamy risotto with a nutty brown ale. Chocolate tart with Belgian cherry beer (kriek). Imperial stout and ice cream—in fact, one of my favorite ever combinations is to pour a strong, thick imperial stout into a shot glass and top it with a tiny scoop of ice cream. It looks like a miniature pint of Guinness, and it feels like white satin and black velvet on the tongue.

That's it—that's all the advice I'm going to offer on the food front, although to get you started, each group of beers in the following pages has a food pairing suggested for the featured beer. This isn't meant to be a definitive match, but it will give you an idea of how the flavors, textures, and intensities of beer and food can work with each other. As with learning about beer, the only way to enjoy is to experiment. For all I know, sardines and sweet stout are a good match—there are endless combinations, so start having some fun with them. But if you want a beer and food match to get you started on the first chapter of tasting notes, I'd suggest tortilla chips with fresh salsa—a great snack food and terrific with cold golden lagers.

food pairing suggestions at a glance

Food	Serving style	Beer suggestion
Beef, pork	Grilled or barbecued	IPA, American pale ale, brown ale
Roast pork	Cold, in sandwiches	kölsch, weissebier
Beef, lamb, chicken	Served in creamy curry sauce	wheat beer, IPA
Cold meats	Sliced, deli-style; or cold pies	pilsner, English ale
Fish, seafood	Fried or broiled, served with a squeeze of lemon	pilsner, bitter
Hard cheeses	Served alone at the end of a meal	barley wine, brown ale
Pizza	With garlic bread and salad	pilsner, Vienna lager

Often, beer goes well with simple fare local to its brewery, such as this English pasty and local golden ale

lager—the global giant

A man walks into a pub, and asks for a beer. The chances are that he'll be handed a lager. Wherever you go in the world, when you ask for "a beer," lager is almost certainly what you will be given. It is a style that has traveled a long way, both geographically and stylistically. Lager (which we now take to mean any beer brewed only with water, malt, hops, and bottom-fermenting yeast) was originally a dark beer—malting technology and techniques did not permit pale malt to be produced. Most malt was roasted brown or black, meaning that the resulting beers were also dark.

The word "lager" is German in origin, and it means "to store." The oft-repeated tale of beer being stored in cold mountain caves, emerging months later much improved, is how the technique of lagering was born. Lagering is essentially a long slow fermentation, during which time the yeast slowly works at the fermentable sugar in the beer. It is the slowness and duration of this process that produces the crisp, clean flavors in a good lager—even the best black lagers have a smooth, clean crispness to them. Faster fermentation, or allowing the yeast to work at a warmer temperature, results in lots of fruity, flowery flavors. These are what you want in an ale, but they have no place in a classic lagerbier.

Good lager takes a long time to make—certainly weeks, and perhaps even months. There is no shortcut to the end product, no substitute for that long, slow lagering process. Any lager that can be produced quickly will have been compromised at some point. That's not to say that a lager produced quickly, or on a large scale, is bad beer, but it's worth knowing that a long, slow production process usually equates to better-tasting lager. Put bluntly, if you pay a bit more, you'll have a more flavorful lager.

The classic style of golden lager is pilsner. Classically, pilsner should be made from pale malt, bottom-fermenting yeast, and, for that extra touch of authenticity, hopped with one of the noble hop varieties (Saaz, Hallertau, Tettnanger, and Spalt). These hops give aroma without excessive bitterness. The resulting beer is all about the medium-bodied balance (neither too light or too forceful) between sweet pale malt and dry, softly bitter hops. That's what good pilsner is. It's more than a word on a label that suggests a beer is fizzy and yellow; it's a style of beer with a very definite archetype, with a very strong sense of time and place. Sure, any lager will wash away the dust on a hot day, but it can't make you stop and savor the moment in the way that a good pilsner does.

pilsner

Pilsner is the classic expression of the golden, sparkling lager that we know today. The beers shown here are great representatives of that style, based as they are on the first golden lagers brewed in the Czech town of Plze (Pilsen, hence "pilsner"). They are mostly light-bodied but have a soft, malty roundness to them, followed by a dry and gently bitter hop finish. Dry, hoppy pilsners are great aperitif beers and can be good all-rounders for many foods. And let's not forget that you can also just drink them; served cold from a fridge on a hot day, nothing else quite hits the spot.

Picturesque Pilsner Urquell Brewery in the Czech Republic

Jever Pilsener

The strongly grassy aroma of this very pale pilsner reminds some of cats, or even skunks. It's true that this is a well-hopped lager, with only a passing impression of pale malt on the palate before the drying hop bitterness of the finish kicks in. Enjoyably austere.

Food match: robust snack food—ham, salami, or fried or tempura shrimp with a squeeze of lemon

Country: Germany
ABV: 4.9%; Serving temp.: 48-50°

AB-Inbev Staropramen

Pouring a lovely burnished gold color, Staropramen has an appetizing aroma—pale malt, a yeasty spiciness, and a hint of citrus pith (grapefruit?) in the mix. In the mouth, a textbook example of a pilsner—sweet pale malt followed by a gently bitter Saaz hop kick. Great balance.
Country: Czech Republic
ABV: 5%; Serving temp.: 48-50°

Schönram Pils

A very pale golden pilsner, with a nice grainy pale malt aroma and a spicy hop note. In the mouth, the hop character is much more pronounced, although still balanced. The hops come to the fore even more in the drying finish, with a long, persistent bitterness.
Country: Germany
ABV: 5%; Serving temp.: 48-55°

Zatecky Pivovar Zatec

There's a good depth of flavor and a surprising amount going on in this golden pilsner. Although the aroma doesn't give much away, the palate has a nice grainy sweetness, while the finish slides elegantly from malty sweetness to a faintly phenolic, bitter dryness.
Country: Czech Republic
ABV: 4.6%; Serving temp.: 48-50°

Dinkelacker-Schwaben Meister Pils

The Tettnang hops used in this beer are detectable as a spicy note in the aroma, and after a little sweetness mid-palate, appear as a dry, grassy note in the enjoyably bitter finish.
Country: Germany
ABV: 4.9%; Serving temp.: 44-48°

lager—the global giant   63

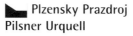 Budweiser Budvar

This beer is literally a national institution in the Czech Republic; the state has partial ownership of the brewery. There is a grassy hop aroma and some nice grain character on the nose, while the palate strikes an even balance between finesse and robustness.

Food match: boiled ham, fried fish, but great on its own

Country: Czech Republic
ABV: 5%; Serving temp.: 44–48°

LIGHT   DARK

LIGHT-BODIED   FULL-BODIED

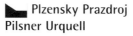 Plzensky Prazdroj Pilsner Urquell

There is a lovely Saaz hop snap to the aroma of this classic pale golden pilsner, with a little grainy malt in support. On the tongue, the beer has a fantastically soft, rounded quality. The sweet vanilla taste on the swallow is slowly replaced with a dry, balanced bitterness.

Country: Czech Republic
ABV: 4.4%; Serving temp.: 44–48°

LIGHT   DARK

LIGHT-BODIED   FULL-BODIED

 Brauerei Hirt Hirter Privat Pils

Not all beers have to be flashy to be great, and Hirter Privat Pils is a good example. A pale golden lager, with a soft grainy aroma, a nice sappy bittersweetness on the palate, and a gently drying finish of medium length. A classic, well-executed beer.

Country: Austria
ABV: 5.2%; Serving temp.: 46–48°

LIGHT   DARK

LIGHT-BODIED   FULL-BODIED

 Stieglbrauerei Stiegl Bier

The nice grainy presence to the pale malt aroma of this mid-gold lager carries into the surprisingly full-bodied palate. There is a good, rounded maltiness—fairly sweet, slightly sappy, with some pleasant grassy hop notes in the finish.

Country: Austria
ABV: 4.9%; Serving temp.: 46–48°

LIGHT   DARK

LIGHT-BODIED   FULL-BODIED

 Heineken Krusovice Imperial

The aroma from this golden beer has a slight hint of vanilla. On the tongue, the grainy quality takes on a slightly more creamy aspect, with the palate dominated by sweetish pale malt. A little hop bitterness builds in the finish, which is rounded and balanced.

Country: Czech Republic
ABV: 5%; Serving temp.: 46–48°

LIGHT   DARK

LIGHT-BODIED   FULL-BODIED

Historic central European Pilsen brewery

A Bavarian man enjoys a large glass of refreshing pilsner

Warsteiner Premium

Germany doesn't have many national brands. However, this is one of the few. Pale toasted malt and a little hop spice on the nose; a soft, sappy sweetness mid-palate; and a gently bitter finish with a good persistence.

Food match: light hors d'oeuvres or a good all-round appetizer

Country: Germany

ABV: 4.8%; Serving temp.: 44-48°

Rakovnik Bakalar Premium

While it doesn't necessarily have the finesse of some other Czech pilsners, there is a good-natured raucousness to this mid-gold lager. Vanilla and apple on the nose, a pale malt sweetness dominates the palate until the hops show up late in the day to slap everything into shape.

Country: Czech Republic

ABV: 5%; Serving temp.: 46-48°

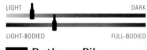

Rothaus Pils

While this very tasty pilsner doesn't reach the hoppy heights that others achieve, a clean, lemony hop note is prevalent throughout. A slight bubblegum note to the nose, bitter hops on the palate, and a sweetish finish showing both malt sweetness and grassy hop bitterness.

Country: Germany

ABV: 5.1%; Serving temp.: 44-48°

Kulmbacher Monchshof Landbier

German beer has an extraordinary number of delineations on a basic style of beer, and landbier is yet another variation on the basic pilsner theme. This example has a spicy, grassy aroma; a slight note of toasted grain; a medium-sweet palate; and a clean, grassy finish. Uncomplicated but enjoyable.

Country: Germany

ABV: 5.4%; Serving temp.: 48-50°

Furstenberg Export

Furstenberg is a pale golden lager displaying a classic balance that adds up to more than the sum of its parts. The grainy aroma has just the faintest suggestion of orange blossom about it, and the clean, crisp, bittersweet body finishes with a hint of pear drops.

Country: Germany

ABV: 5.3%; Serving temp.: 45-48°

lager—the global giant   67

"new wave" pilsner

There are some slightly more unusual examples of pilsners in this spread—indeed, some stretch the definition to breaking point. Birrificio Italiano's Tipopils is hazy and yeasty, which pilsner purists frown upon—"proper" pilsner is clear and golden. The color of Prima Pils won't be a problem, but the fresh lemony aromas might cause a few eyebrows to be raised. And the hop-load in Christoffel Blonde is the pilsner equivalent of throwing a lighted match into a box of fireworks.

After a hard day working Pennsylvania's farmland, one of Victory's beers provides perfect refreshment

🇮🇹 Birrificio Italiano Tipopils

The sensational fresh aroma on this hazy golden pilsner is treat enough on its own—pale malt, toasted grain, fresh bread, grassy hops, and a hint of lemon. But there's more; the sappy, bittersweet palate has an incredible texture, and the bitter, bready finish demands another mouthful. Unfiltered, unpasteurized, unbeatable.

Food match: bruschetta or crostini, pizza, or simple pasta dishes
Country: Italy
ABV: 5.2%; Serving temp.: 46–50°

🇺🇸 Victory Prima Pils

This pale golden lager is something really special. The crisp, lemon zest nose has a lovely noble hop character, with some vanilla notes. Pale malt is evident throughout, layered with gently bitter hops and more citrus zest. A little grapefruit pops up in the finish. Very good indeed.
Country: USA
ABV: 5.3%; Serving temp.: 48–50°

➕ Samuel Smith's Pure Brewed Lager

Although best known for their ales, the iconic Samuel Smith's also produces good lagers. This example has a lovely delicacy, somewhere between a kölsch and a pilsner, with a citrus note to the nose; a fresh, clean palate; and a clean, balanced finish.
Country: England
ABV: 5%; Serving temp.: 40–45°

🇺🇸 Gordon Biersch Pilsner

From a brewery majoring in classic German styles, this pilsner has a soft, grainy nose, with some lemony hop notes; a full, slightly sweet palate; and a finish that treads the classic balance between sweet and dry. Malt and lemony hops show far into the finish.
Country: USA
ABV: 5.3%; Serving temp.: 48–50°

🇳🇱 Christoffel Blonde

There's a splendid, resinous, spicy intensity to the aroma of this innocuous-looking beer that would be at home in an American pale ale. Bitter (but somehow juicy) Saaz hops dominate the flavor, although there is a supporting malt sweetness in the tangy, bitter finish.
Country: Holland
ABV: 6%; Serving temp.: 46–50°

lager—the global giant 69

pilsner-style lager

While pilsners are the classic expression of the lager style, pilsner-style lagers are beers that are broadly in the same style but don't have quite the requisite body and intensity to pass themselves off as the real thing. But that's not to say these are bad beers; rather, they are more about slaking a thirst under the holiday sun or acting as a setting for a night's socializing. It's true that life's too short to drink boring beer, but conversely, not every beer that you drink has to be a world-beating classic.

Copper mash tun used to brew pilsner-style lager

Heineken Export

Let's be honest, Heineken isn't about to voted "best beer in the world." But there's a soft graininess, a hint of lemon, and a gentle hop dryness that in the right place, at the right time, are hard to beat. A macrobrew, no doubt, but one of the better ones out there.

Food match: none needed, but potato chips if you like or salsa with tortilla chips

Country: Holland
ABV: 5%; Serving temp.: 39–46°

Lindeboom Pilsener

Pale gold in color, Lindeboom has a classic lager sweet corn note to the pale grain aroma, alongside a delicate hop note. Lively on the palate, there is a nice bitterness to the finish, which also has a pleasant lemony spritz. Finish is snappy and dry.
Country: Holland
ABV: 5%; Serving temp.: 44–48°

LIGHT ▮ DARK
LIGHT-BODIED ▮ FULL-BODIED

Hahn Premium

Although large-production beers are generally synonymous with lower quality, this pale, delicate, pilsner-style beer has a soft maltiness running through it, coupled with a grassy bitterness derived from the Hersbrucker hop. This is an Australian lager with a distinct German accent.
Country: Australia
ABV: 5%; Serving temp.: 35–41°

Mythos Mythos

Mythos is a holiday beer par excellence; under the Hellenic sun, it tastes flowery and honeyed, with a nice balanced bitterness to the finish. Away from its home turf, it's still a perfectly decent, well-structured lager, with a good pilsner-style bitterness to the finish.
Country: Greece
ABV: 4.7%; Serving temp.: 35–41°

LIGHT ▮ DARK
LIGHT-BODIED ▮ FULL-BODIED

Gösser Export

A note of hop-derived lemon sherbet runs through this golden lager, and very appealing it is too. Grainy on the nose, with a nice spritzy quality to the palate. The finish is initially dry and lemony, with a little toasted nutty grain peeking through later on.
Country: Austria
ABV: 5.2%; Serving temp.: 45–48°

lager—the global giant   71

 Kross Pilsner

Pilsner it ain't, but there is an appealing floral and citrus note on the nose of this golden lager. A little grainy sweetness makes a brief appearance mid-palate before the hops kick in with more floral and citrus notes in the dry finish. Surprisingly tasty.

Food match: ceviche, or any broiled seafood with a squeeze of lemon
Country: Chile
ABV: 4.9%; Serving temp.: 44–48°

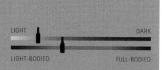

Krönleins Crocodile

Despite giving the impression of trading on past glories by displaying a gold medal won over a decade ago, this is a pretty decent effort. A nice, uncomplicated note of lemon sherbet and pine needles runs though the aroma and flavor of this mid-gold lager.
Country: Sweden
ABV: 5.2%; Serving temp.: 44–48°

Alhambra 1925 Reserva

From the copper-gold color, to the assertive nose of toasted malt, honey, and a rounded fruitiness, to the sweetish palate that dries with a slightly medicinal edge and more toasted grain notes, this is a thoroughly enjoyable beer.
Country: Spain
ABV: 6.4%; Serving temp.: 44–48°

Pietra Pietra

Mid-gold in color, Pietra has a grainy aroma overlaid with some autumnal spiciness. On the tongue, there is a nice firmness to the body and an almost smoky note to the palate. The finish is dry, with a nutty quality, perhaps derived from the chestnut flour used in the fermentation.
Country: France
ABV: 6%; Serving temp.: 44–48

Moritz Moritz

There's a lot of work going on around the Moritz brand at the time of writing, including building a brewpub in Barcelona. There's a nice lightness to this pale beer, but that doesn't mean it's bland; a soft lemon sherbet character pervades this bright, clean, and fresh lager.
Country: Spain
ABV: 5.5%; Serving temp.: 44–48°

Beer barrels used for storing and transporting lager and other keg beers

Rows of hops growing in New Zealand

 Monteith's New Zealand Lager

There's a hint of caramel and ripe apple to the aroma of this mid-golden lager. The palate has a grainy malt sweetness, and the finish has a good fruity quality (more yellow apple) that becomes dry and softly bitter in the finish. Perfectly decent, if not earth-shaking.

Food match: oddly, marinated artichoke hearts with brie are good with this
Country: New Zealand
ABV: 5%; Serving temp.: 44–48°

 Heineken Zagorka Special

There's a whiff of pear drops on the nose of this Bulgarian lager, and a heady quality too (minty?). In the mouth, the unexpected fruitiness continues with ripe apples and a hint of vanilla. The sweetish finish could use a bit of bitterness. Unusual, but fine in a pinch.
Country: Bulgaria
ABV: 5%; Serving temp.: 44–48°

LIGHT | DARK
LIGHT-BODIED | FULL-BODIED

● Sapporo Premium

A pale malt note is detectable on the nose of this golden lager, and fruity esters give a fleeting impression of ripe yellow apples, layered under spicy hops. The palate is fairly full, with an almost oily texture, and the finish is initially sweet, becoming slightly drier.
Country: Japan
ABV: 4.7%; Serving temp.: 44–48°

 Krakus Zywiec

There is a pronounced cereal aroma to this Polish beer from the Krakus Brewery. The sweetish palate has a nice weight, with almost an oily quality, and a hint of butterscotch or banana to the bittersweet finish. Firmly in the commercial camp, but none the worse for it.
Country: Poland
ABV: 5.6%; Serving temp.: 44–48°

LIGHT | DARK
LIGHT-BODIED | FULL-BODIED

◾ Taybeh Golden

Proof that, with determination, you can make beer pretty much anywhere (although Taybeh sold in Europe is brewed in Belgium). An all-malt golden lager, with a grassy hop edge, some fruitiness (ripe apples), and a clean finish. Somewhat incongruously, they hold an annual Oktoberfest.
Country: Palestine
ABV: 5.5%; Serving temp.: 44–48°

lager—the global giant 75

🇦🇺 Carlton & United Victoria Bitter

"VB" is one of those beers that inspires tremendous loyalty in its fans. While it isn't an English-style bitter, it does have a nice crunchy hop character wrapped around a pale malt core. Very little sweetness at all, with a fairly long, fairly dry finish. Fair dinkum, as they say.

Food match: follow the locals—drink this while shrimp cook on the barbie

Country: Australia
ABV: 4.8%; Serving temp.: 44–48°

▪▪ Peroni Nastro Azzurro

Perhaps trading on its Italian style rather than its ingredients, Nastro Azzurro is an increasingly popular beer and a perfectly decent example of a commercial Mediterranean lager. A clean, grainy nose with a hint of vanilla, while the light, slightly phenolic finish has a nice, tart bitterness.
Country: Italy
ABV: 5.1%; Serving temp.: 44–48°

▪ Hacker-Pschorr Münchner Gold

There's something about the beers from this Munich brewery that sets them apart. Even this relatively humble export-style lager has a wonderful spritzy cleanness, from the soft grainy aroma to the dry finish, which has a hint of toasted grain.
Country: Germany
ABV: 5.5%; Serving temp.: 44–48°

▪▪ AB-Inbev Stella Artois

It's hard to be objective about such an omnipresent brand. The original is decent enough. Pale gold, with a balanced nose (sweet malt and hops both in evidence), a rounded palate, and a medium-length spicy finish. Foreign-brewed versions can vary from the original.
Country: Belgium
ABV: 5.2%; Serving temp.: 44–48°

▬ Grolsch Grolsch Premium

Unless you've been to Holland, this is the only Grolsch beer that you're likely to know (well, maybe their excellent weizen too). This no-nonsense golden lager has all the attributes of a pils—soft grassy aroma, sweetly malty, a gentle bitterness in the finish.
Country: Holland
ABV: 5%; Serving temp.: 44–48°

Traditional German beer stein used for celebratory drinking

Horseshoe Falls in Tasmania, the pure water source for James Boag's Premium

🇦🇺 James Boag's Premium

There is an aroma of malt and cereal to this golden beer, which some drinkers enjoy and others find a little off-putting. It would be a shame to be put off, though, as the palate has a lovely light, slightly floral quality and a clean, airy freshness to the finish.

Food match: a delicate drinking beer, so ordinary bar snacks are a safe bet
Country: Australia
ABV: 5%; Serving temp.: 44–48°

● Asahi Dry

Asahi is such a big brand in Japan that it has no "home" brewery; there are several across the country, and contract breweries all around the world. This UK-brewed sample, as the name suggests, has a little malt sweetness, and a balanced, dry hoppiness throughout.
Country: Japan
ABV: 5%; Serving temp.: 44–48°

▬ Mahou Cinco Estrellas

Although there is little in its golden appearance and grainy aroma to distinguish it from similar beers, there is a certain weight to the palate that sets it apart. It has a robust tartness and an almost nutty note on the tongue, and a nice bitter finish.
Country: Spain
ABV: 5.5%; Serving temp.: 44–48°

➕ Hartwall Lapin Kulta

Hailing from Lapland, this pale golden beer has a soft grain aroma that leads to a medium-bodied, slightly sweet palate. There is a nice weight and mouthfeel, and the finish is clean, with some grassy bitterness in the aftertaste.
Country: Finland
ABV: 4.5%; Serving temp.: 44–48°

● Kirin Ichiban

Utilizing the "Ichiban Shibori" brewing method, where only the "first pressings" of the wort are fermented. One would expect this to produce a very strong malty beer, but somehow what comes out is a rounded golden lager, with a little citrus hop character in the finish.
Country: Japan
ABV: 5%; Serving temp.: 44–48°

lager—the global giant **79**

asian lager

These lagers (perhaps Tiger to a lesser extent) all hang together as a cohesive group by virtue of using rice as an ingredient. It's not uncommon for a brewery to use a non-malt adjunct as a source of fermentable sugar, and in these beers, the slightly sweet, almost perfumed note that it gives is quite evident. It used to be the case that "adjunct" was synonymous with "cheap," although that is no longer the case. These breweries use rice not to cut costs, but to deliver a distinct flavor.

Beer barrels preserved in an ancient Chinese brewery

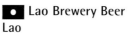 ## Tsingtao Tsingtao

With rice unashamedly listed as an ingredient alongside the usual quartet, it's hard to avoid imagining that you can smell it on the nose. The palate too has a distinctive Asian note— green tea, perhaps? A gentle hop bitterness and green tea note pervade into the finish.

Food match: a good pan-Asian standby, best with less sweet food

Country: China
ABV: 4.7%; Serving temp.: 48°

Lao Brewery Beer Lao

Beer Lao has an indefinable but distinctly Asian quality. Perhaps it is the slightly floral, almost phenolic, honeyed aroma, or the slightly sweet jasmine tea note on the tongue. Either way, brewed with Laotian rice, this modest golden lager has a definite sense of place to it.
Country: Laos
ABV: 5%; Serving temp.: 44–48°

Singha Premium

There seem to be two versions of this pale golden beer in the market at present. The stronger version is as good as ever, with a firm, malty body and a perfumed, floral hop finish. The 5%abv version is nice enough, though a little thinner and less assertive.
Country: Thailand
ABV: 5%; Serving temp.: 48°

Chang Export

Chang falls happily into the classic style for lagers from this region. A pale gold lager with a slightly floral, honeyed note on the nose and a clean, reasonably crisp palate, with some floral notes poking through the lightly bitter finish. Tastes amazing on a sunny beach, I would imagine.
Country: Thailand
ABV: 5%; Serving temp.: 44–48°

Asia Pacific Tiger

The delicately pale malty sweetness, light bitterness, and slightly bready finish of Tiger beer makes perfect sense in the heat and humidity of Singapore. Although unashamedly commercial, and not the most flavorful of beers, it's an icon for its home country.
Country: Singapore
ABV: 5%; Serving temp.: 36–40°

lager—the global giant 81

"un-lager"

This is really a made-up grouping of lagers, but they are all somehow a little bit different. The first two are unfiltered— basically, they are cloudy beers. This gives them a depth of flavor, and perhaps a slightly fuller body, than their filtered equivalents. Keo is unpasteurized, and as a result tastes a bit livelier. Both Svaneke Sejlor Øl and Kasteel Cru are fermented with champagne yeast, an unusual ingredient that makes them particularly tasty.

A quiet glass of lager is part of European café culture

 Schremser Roggen Bio Bier

Copper-colored and fairly hazy, this has the graininess of a lager mixed with the fruity spiciness of a wheat beer on the nose. On the palate, weissebier fruitiness is evident (banana, ripe apple) along with some faint spiciness (mace?). Finish is soft, rounded, and fruity. Organic, unfiltered.

Food match: honey-roast pork and spaetzle

Country: Austria
ABV: 5.2%; Serving temp.: 48–50°

 Bernard Kvasnicove Svetly Lezak

"Kvasnicove" indicates a cloudy pilsner. The correct technique is to leave the beer unfiltered, though some producers filter and then re-add yeast. Bernard does the right thing, resulting in a softly hazy lager with a yeasty spiciness and the vitality associated with good English ale.
Country: Czech Republic
ABV: 5.1%; Serving temp.: 48°

Coors Kasteel Cru

There is an appealing tartness to the nose of this very pale lager, almost reminiscent of the acetic note in a lambic. On the palate, a lemony dryness dominates, with very little malt character, save for a crackerlike bite in the dry finish. A good, spritzy beer.
Country: France
ABV: 5.2%; Serving temp.: 40–42°

 Keo Keo

This Cypriot beer is unpasteurized, preserving a certain delicacy that other lagers of a similar strength simply don't have. There is a slightly honeyed note to the aroma and a softly floral note to the palate. Dry, short finish. Not a world-beater, but nice enough nonetheless.
Country: Cyprus
ABV: 4.5%; Serving temp.: 44–48°

Svaneke Sejlor Øl

When I met the brewer of Svaneke, I asked him which was his favorite beer in his portfolio. He unhesitatingly reached for this light but tasty and fresh lager, given an extra edge with some champagne yeast fermentation. He was right to—it's a real treat.
Country: Denmark
ABV: 3.3%; Serving temp.: 44–48°

helles & helles-bock

I was in a beer store recently and noticed two customers pointing and laughing at the label of the Andechs Spezial Hell listed here. "I'm not buying that," one of them commented, "it sends you to your own special hell." It's true, it might if you drank enough of it, but hell isn't a warning, it's a description—it's the German word for "pale." Bock attached to the first word denotes a stronger beer—we'll see more bock beers a little further on, along with their relatives, the doppelbocks.

Crowds of beer enthusiasts drinking at Oktoberfest

■ Hacker-Pschorr Superior Festbier

A light toffee note sits happily alongside the more usual grain aroma of this golden lager. The palate has a noticeable weight, an almost buttery texture, and a medium-bodied finish with a faint caramel taste and a hint of alcohol warmth.

Food match: braised pork chops with slow-cooked onions

Country: Germany
ABV: 6%; Serving temp.: 44–48°

■ Trunk Vierzehnheiligen Silberbock Hell

A bright, golden beer with a sappy sweetness. The aroma is full of pale grain, with a hint of butterscotch and pear drops (not strictly appropriate to the style, but appealing). Slightly sticky mouthfeel, with a lovely rounded sweetness developing in the finish.
Country: Germany
ABV: 6.8%; Serving temp.: 44–48°

■ Paulaner Original Münchner Hell

The softly rounded quality of this delicate hell has many devotees. The gently malty aroma has just a suggestion of the hopsack about it, while the light body has a sweet, slightly sappy quality. Bitterness in the medium-dry finish is fairly low.
Country: Germany
ABV: 4.9%; Serving temp.: 48°

■ Andechs Spezial Hell

Even the relatively ordinary beers from this excellent brewery are a little bit spezial. The faintly hazy gold color has a wholesome look, and the aroma of sweet pale malt has an appetizing fruitiness (ripe apples). Rounded in the mouth, with a bittersweet finish.
Country: Germany
ABV: 5.9%; Serving temp.: 44–48°

■ Dinkelacker-Schwaben Privat

At first try, it seems as though there isn't a great deal going on here. The aroma is perhaps a bit too grainy to be totally appetizing, but press on to the medium-dry palate and finish with its tangy hop bitterness, and it makes a bit more sense.
Country: Germany
ABV: 5.1%; Serving temp.: 41–45°

märzen/oktoberfest

If you're reading this while drinking a beer, you might just want
to put it down and pay attention, as this is a little complicated.
Märzen are beers that, traditionally, are brewed for the Munich
Oktoberfest. They are brewed in March (März in German)
and ferment slowly, and then are bottled or kegged for
consumption in September. That's right, Oktoberfest begins in September.
Are you still following this? Good. Märzen are traditionally copper-gold in color,
robustly malty, with a little supporting hop character. Plain Oktoberfestbier is often just a
stronger version of a normal beer, hence the inclusion of a robust Czech pilsner here.

A Bavarian woman in traditional costume sells Lebkuchen hearts at Oktoberfest

Hacker-Pschorr Oktoberfest Märzen

It seems as though proper märzen for Oktoberfest have fallen out of fashion, but Hacker-Pschorr carry the standard with this lovely copper-colored beer. The assertively malty aroma has a touch of caramel, while the palate is full-bodied and medium-sweet, with a dry nuttiness in the finish.

Food match: bratwurst with sauerkraut, or (if ravenous) a classic choucroute

Country: Germany
ABV: 5.8%; Serving temp.: 45–50°

Rothaus Märzen

This lively golden märzen has a nice full-bodied quality, with some toasted grain notes on the nose and a faint orchard fruit accent. Slightly sweet on the palate, with some toffee and ripe apple notes, which carry into the fairly sweet, rounded finish.
Country: Germany
ABV: 5.6%; Serving temp.: 45–50°

Dinkelacker-Schwaben Märzen

Although rather pale for a märzen, this golden beer has a pleasantly robust quality. The aroma has nice grain presence, with a faint hint of alcohol. The beer is full-bodied and sweetish, with some dryness and a little bitterness in the rich finish.
Country: Germany
ABV: 5.6%; Serving temp.: 48°

Gordon Biersch Märzen

This has the classic märzen copper-orange color and a distinct caramel note on the nose. The body has a soft sweetness, with some textbook nutty malt and a little more medium-dry caramel flavor on the palate, augmented by a little grassy hoppiness in the finish.
Country: USA
ABV: 5.7%; Serving temp.: 48°

Bohemia Regent Prezident

Alongside the pale malt aroma of this beer is a suggestion of ripe fruit (banana? pear?). There is an appealing sapidity to the palate, with a lively fruity note dancing alongside the pale malt. The finish becomes gradually drier, with a gentle hop bite.
Country: Czech Republic
ABV: 6%; Serving temp.: 40–45°

vienna lager

Stylistically, Vienna lager and märzen are quite closely related. In truth, there isn't much to separate them, but for the sake of form, I've arbitrarily drawn a line and placed the following beers in the Vienna category. As a group, they all exhibit fuller, darker malt character than a regular märzen and are a good deal more flavorful and robust too. The Austrian link is Viennese brewer Anton Dreher, who around 1840 created clear bronze-colored beers en route to producing golden lagers. These inspired Munich brewer Gabriel Sedlmayr to produce the same style for Oktoberfest.

Exceptional when served at 2°

FREEDOM

ABV 4.7%

LAGER

The carnival atmosphere of Coney Island in Brooklyn inspired Shmaltz's "freakshow" beers

 Brooklyn Lager

A modern interpretation of the Vienna style, this copper-colored example has an enjoyably assertive hop aroma (orange and grapefruit). The palate is medium-dry, with a brief burst of malt before the hops come crackling back into play, finishing medium-dry and tangerine-like.

Food match: the brewery markets this as a perfect match for pizza

Country: USA
ABV: 5.2%; Serving temp.: 44-48°

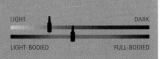

Christoffel Robertus

Christoffel Robertus has a lovely ruby-amber color, and a slight haze if poured from the bottle. There is a good fruit aroma (overripe banana) alongside a malted milk note and a faint whiff of alcohol. On the palate is a slightly nutty malt quality in the sweetish finish.

Country: Holland
ABV: 6%; Serving temp.: 45-50°

✚ Freedom Organic Dark Lager

Dark lagers tend to be black, but this is coppery red. There is a lovely toasted grain aroma, with some notes of toffee, medium-sweet mid-palate (figs), and dry finish, although without obvious hop character. A classic Vienna lager from an unexpected source.

Country: England
ABV: 4.7%; Serving temp.: 48-50°

Modelo Negra Modelo

There's a mellow, fruity aroma to this deep copper-colored lager. On the palate, a soft maltiness prevails, with hints of toffee and darker dried fruit. The finish is rounded and sweet, with notes of milk chocolate and cola. Smooth, sweetish, and very enjoyable.

Country: Mexico
ABV: 5.3%; Serving temp.: 48-50°

Shmaltz Coney Island Lager

Robust floral and citrus hops overlay a malt backbone, which gives a nutty character to the beer in the same way the sun gives our solar system something to spin around. Almost like brown ale, this is sweet, big, and chewy, finishing nutty and bittersweet.

Country: USA
ABV: 5.5%; Serving temp.: 40-45°

lager—the global giant   89

lager oddments

A few loose bottles that I can't seem to squeeze in anywhere else—help yourself, they're all good. The two dunkel are dark lagers—one sweeter, one drier—that form a link from the previous Vienna lagers to the bocks, doppelbocks, and black lagers later in this section. Sam Adams Boston Lager has ended up here because it's stylistically close to a Vienna lager, and it's a beer that has turned lots of people on to the world of craft beer. The honey lager, though a bit of an oddity, is certainly worth trying.

Statue of Samuel Adams, American hero and inspiration for Boston Lager

🇺🇸 Samuel Adams Boston Lager

For many, the copper-colored Boston Lager is the "gateway" beer that opens up the world of craft brewing. On the nose, floral hops dominate, with a little caramel malt also evident. The medium-dry palate has toffee and cracker notes, with a perfumed note returning on the finish.

Food match: broiled hot dogs, mustard, and onions, for a perfect Boston tea party

Country: USA
ABV: 4.8%; Serving temp.: 40-44°

▪ Schönram Original Altbayerisch Dunkel

Copper-brown, with a creamy head so persistent that it seems nitrogenated (it's not). The delicate aroma is of toffee and coffee, with spiciness and a hint of nuts. Lovely silky texture, low carbonation, finishing dry with some dark fruit notes. Soft, rounded, and very enjoyable.
Country: Germany
ABV: 5%; Serving temp.: 48-55°

LIGHT ———————————————— DARK

LIGHT-BODIED ———————————— FULL-BODIED

▪ Weltenburger Kloster Winter-Traum

This copper-gold beer is an exercise in restraint. Nothing about it is particularly showy, but falling as it does somewhere between a hell and a bock, it combines the easy drinkability of the first with the nutty, fruity malt character of the second. A lovely winter special.
Country: Germany
ABV: 5.4%; Serving temp.: 48-50°

LIGHT ———————————————— DARK

LIGHT-BODIED ———————————— FULL-BODIED

▬ Schremser Doppelmalz

Very dark brown, with red highlights, this beer has a grainy aroma close to a Czech dark lager, but with less coffee and chocolate and more juicy, fruity malt. Sweet on the palate, with caramel and honey notes. Toasted, grassy dryness in the finish.
Country: Austria
ABV: 4.5%; Serving temp.: 45-50°

LIGHT ———————————————— DARK

LIGHT-BODIED ———————————— FULL-BODIED

🇺🇸 High Falls JW Dundee Honey Brown

This amber lager has an added slug of honey that, while it doesn't make it the most exciting beer ever, does at least give it a bit of character. A floral and caramel aroma, a sweetish palate, and a slightly sweet, floral finish, with a faint nuttiness.
Country: USA
ABV: 4.5%; Serving temp.: 35-40°

LIGHT ———————————————— DARK

LIGHT-BODIED ———————————— FULL-BODIED

black lager

Although it's hard to believe it, all lager was once black (or very dark brown) and often quite murky. How different the culture of beer appreciation would be if this were still the case. Instead of enjoying the way the light shines though a bright, clear glass of golden pilsner, we might instead marvel at how our beer manages to block out the light. Perhaps rather than returning a beer to the bar for being a little cloudy, we would return it for being too clear. Times change, but luckily we can still find black lager if we look hard enough.

Black lager brewing vessels in a Bohemian brewery

Kaltenberg König Ludwig Dunkel

Brewed by a prince, but fit for a king (König in German), this dark reddish-brown is brewed by Prince Luitpold of Bavaria in honor of his regal forebears. Faintly smoky, with notes of dates and coffee on the nose; smooth and richly textured on the palate; medium-dry finish.

Food match: roast or broiled pork with caramelized onions and applesauce

Country: Germany
ABV: 5.1%; Serving temp.: 48°

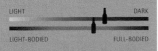

Jever Dark

There is a really wholesome roasted grain aroma to this ruddy-dark lager, alongside an herbal note (presumably hop-derived, but it smells like roasted chicory coffee). Balanced mouthfeel, leading to a nutty, roast malt finish. Fresh and uncomplicated, but enjoyable.
Country: Germany
ABV: 4.9%; Serving temp.: 42-48°

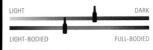

Köstritzer Schwarzbier

This dark mahogany lager gives off a roasted grain aroma, which has an almost savory quality. The palate has a creamy smoothness that doesn't rely on nitro-widgets, and although relatively light-bodied, there is a gentle intensity to the chocolate and dried fruit in the finish.
Country: Germany
ABV: 4.8%; Serving temp.: 48°

Dinkelacker-Schwaben Das Schwarze

The nice depth of roasted grain aroma of this schwarzbier is reminiscent of chestnuts roasting over a coal-fired brazier. The smoky nuttiness persists into the dryish palate, and through into the slightly tart finish, which also displays hints of bitter chocolate and a little hop dryness.
Country: Germany
ABV: 4.9%; Serving temp.: 48°

Bohemia Regent Tmavy

"Tmavy" designates dark beer, and this is indeed a very dark lager, almost black with ruby highlights. It has an aroma of grain and caramel, overlaid with coffee and a little burnt sugar. In the mouth, the surprisingly light body carries more burnt sugar before a shortish, dried fruitcake finish.
Country: Czech Republic
ABV: 4.4%; Serving temp.: 46-50°

lager—the global giant   93

🏴󠁧󠁢󠁳󠁣󠁴󠁿 BrewDog Zeitgeist

BrewDog is trying to style this as its shot at the mainstream. The trouble is, these dandy brewpunks couldn't do mainstream if their lives depended on it. Chocolate, coffee, and grapefruit zest on the nose, more grapefruit on the palate, then a long roasted malt finish with floral twist.

Food match: good on its own, great with slow-cooked ribs

Country: Scotland
ABV: 4.9%; Serving temp.: 46–52°

▬ Obolon Deep Velvet

Naming a beer after something plush and luxurious is asking for trouble, but this dark, sweetish lager wears the burden well. Scorched caramel, grain, and milky coffee on the nose, with a medium-sweet palate, a burst of malty fruit on the swallow, and a nutty toffee finish.
Country: Ukraine
ABV: 5.3%; Serving temp.: 46–52°

◢ Budweiser Budvar Dark

A fruity malt aroma is under-pinned by notes of coffee and dark chocolate in this ruby-brown beer, the dark version of the Czech classic. The initially sweet palate becomes drier and more bitter in the finish, with bitter chocolate and coffee dominating, along with a little Saaz hop bite.
Country: Czech Republic
ABV: 4.7%; Serving temp.: 46–52°

● Asahi Black

Demonstrating that adjunct (rice and maize here) doesn't mean boring beer, this ruddy-brown lager has a fantastic aroma of roast grain, coffee, and dried fruit. The medium-sweet palate is full, with coffee and licorice notes, while the dry, roasty finish has some nice malt loaf character. Very good indeed.
Country: Japan
ABV: 5%; Serving temp.: 46–52°

▬ Alhambra Negra

This very dark beer (the highlights are ruby red) has a lovely aroma of toffee and coffee and a faintly honeyed note. The palate is a little lighter and drier than the aromas suggest, but there is still some good roasted grain and burnt caramel character.
Country: Spain
ABV: 5.4%; Serving temp.: 46–52°

The Asahi building in Tokyo, business center for Japanese black lager

bock & doppelbock

Bock beers take their name from the German town of Einbeck, where they were first brewed in the fourteenth century. It would be easy to describe them as strong lagers, although that would be to sell them somewhat short. As well as being strong, they have a tendency to fruity sweetness, and a rich wholesome quality that is somewhat hard to describe. Even stronger are doppelbock (literally "double bock," although not actually twice as strong), which are also darker and more intense. While the bock beers here are an eclectic international selection, the doppelbock are all authentically German.

Traditional half-timbered houses in Einbeck, Germany, where bock originated

■■ Birrificio Italiano Amber Shock

Sold only in bottles, this hazy copper-colored beer has a lovely estery, fruity nose (banana, orange), nuts, toffee, and a suggestion of alcohol. The palate is medium-sweet, with more fruit (dried apricot, orange), some nuttiness, a hint of cognac, and a medium-sweet, fruity finish.

Food match: odd as it sounds, duck á l'orange would be perfect
Country: Italy
ABV: 7%; Serving temp.: 44–48°

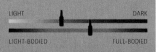

LIGHT ——————— DARK
LIGHT-BODIED ——————— FULL-BODIED

■■ Peroni Gran Riserva

The burnished gold body and slightly higher alcohol content suggest a lager with aspirations above the ordinary, and it succeeds. The malty, grainy nose has a slightly spirity quality, and the assertive palate is mouth-filling and dry, with a pleasantly bitter, pithy note. Crisp, persistent finish. Good quality.
Country: Italy
ABV: 6.6%; Serving temp.: 48°

LIGHT ——————— DARK
LIGHT-BODIED ——————— FULL-BODIED

▬▬ Schloss Eggenberg Urbock 23°

This is the sort of beer you save for a special occasion, and then rashly open as a nightcap after a long day. Well, that's what I've just done anyway. Pin-bright and golden, with an aroma of scorched caramel, pale malt, and cognac. Sweet, slightly peachy, warming alcohol.
Country: Austria
ABV: 9.6%; Serving temp.: 48°

LIGHT ——————— DARK
LIGHT-BODIED ——————— FULL-BODIED

■■ Birrificio Italiano Bibock

A fabulous aroma of nutty malt and bitter oranges wafts from this hazy copper-colored beer, with a faint note of toasted grain husk. Initially sweet, a wave of hops (more bitter orange) sweeps across the tongue, finishing bittersweet, with a full-flavored malt flourish.
Country: Italy
ABV: 6.2%; Serving temp.: 46–50°

LIGHT ——————— DARK
LIGHT-BODIED ——————— FULL-BODIED

▬▬ Gordon Biersch Blonde Bock

Amber-gold in color, with a big malty nose, a sweet spiciness, and a suggestion of alcohol. A wonderful full texture, slightly heavy and almost oily on the palate, with some sweet pale maltiness, a faintly peachy quality, and a little warmth on the swallow. Very enjoyable.
Country: USA
ABV: 7%; Serving temp.: 48–55°

LIGHT ——————— DARK
LIGHT-BODIED ——————— FULL-BODIED

Weltenburger Kloster Asam Bock

Pouring a dark ruddy-brown, there is a soft roasted grain aroma, with some toasted malt loaf character too. The relatively low carbonation lends an easy drinkability, and the coffee and fruitcake notes persist well into the finish. A great beer; one to seek out.

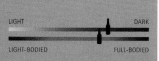

Food match: hearty, earthy food—beef fillet with roast beets and wild mushrooms

Country: Germany
ABV: 6.9%; **Serving temp.:** 48–52°

LIGHT ─────────── DARK
LIGHT-BODIED ─────────── FULL-BODIED

Weihenstephaner Korbinian

This has a big aroma of dried fruit, nutty malt, and a plush quality (aged cognac and sherry casks). In the mouth, caramel, dried fruit, and chocolate flavors combine. The finish is long and becomes medium-dry, with more chocolate and vanilla notes. Complex, deeply satisfying.
Country: Germany
ABV: 7.4%; **Serving temp.:** 48–52°

LIGHT ─────────── DARK
LIGHT-BODIED ─────────── FULL-BODIED

Andechs Doppelbock Dunkel

The nutty, slightly grainy aroma to this dark lager promises good times, and the palate doesn't disappoint either. Sweetly malty, with some coffee liqueur notes and a soft, rounded quality that makes it worryingly easy to drink. Finish is malty and medium-dry.
Country: Germany
ABV: 7.1%; **Serving temp.:** 48–52°

LIGHT ─────────── DARK
LIGHT-BODIED ─────────── FULL-BODIED

Paulaner Salvator

Originally brewed as "liquid bread" sustenance during Lent, Salvator (Latin for "savior") is an orange-brown beer with a luscious, nourishing malt character. Medium-sweet on the palate, with some dried fruit, toffee, and a faint hoppy spiciness. For many, the textbook example of a doppelbock.
Country: Germany
ABV: 7.5%; **Serving temp.:** 48–52°

LIGHT ─────────── DARK
LIGHT-BODIED ─────────── FULL-BODIED

Ayinger Celebrator Doppelbock

This dark beer with ruby highlights is something special. Despite its relatively slight aroma of dried fruit and winter spice, it opens on the palate, and the slightly oily texture reveals flavors of burnt fruitcake and licorice. Roasted grain, rum, and figs pervade the long, dry finish.
Country: Germany
ABV: 6.7%; **Serving temp.:** 48–52°

LIGHT ─────────── DARK
LIGHT-BODIED ─────────── FULL-BODIED

Waitress in historic costume serving a tray of Bavarian beer

english ale, british beer

There is nothing quite like British beer. Even in countries where the influence of British beer has spawned a brewing revolution that has turned into a craft industry (and I'm thinking primarily of the United States here), there is something lost in translation. Although now that I think of it, one of the best pints of bitter (and plate of fish and chips) I ever had was in a brewpub in St. Louis, Missouri, in the early 1990s. I wish I could remember its name—perhaps I shouldn't have kept going back for more.

That's a common problem with good British beer—it's just too drinkable. Although it is relatively modest in strength (ranging mostly from 4% to 6% alcohol by volume), it has a soft, rounded elegance that is unmatched by anything else in the beer pantheon. From the cask, in a pub, where it is mostly found at its best, the lower carbonation and cool (rather than cold) serving temperature means that it can slip down all too easily. In recognition of this drinkability, there is a peculiarly British creation—the session beer. These are lower strength beers that are designed for drinking pleasure, acknowledging that the drinker is likely to want a second or third pint of delicious ale without taking on too much alcohol.

British beer (it is produced all over the United Kingdom and Ireland, and beyond) is a broad church—there are many styles that fall under this catchall term. As with lager and pilsner in the previous chapter, the key is balance. However, the top-fermenting yeasts and range of colored malts that are used to brew this style of ale mean that the end product can be anything from clean, crisp, and golden, to fruity, sweet, and fairly dark. But the sweetness of the malt (whatever its color) and the hop bitterness always work against each other, producing a beer of unusual balance and delicacy.

I have to admit to being a little disingenuous talking about British beer as a single style. There is, for example, quite a bit of difference between a classic English ale and a typical Scottish ale. But although this difference exists, the techniques are largely the same. The end result is shaped more by the environment from where it hails than by anything else. Scottish ales have a tendency to be more robust and sweeter because that is what is popular in a country where the winters can be a little more challenging than those of its southern neighbor. There we have it again—a style of beer as belonging to a particular place, influenced by local factors. With British pale golden ales, there is also a sense of seasonality—a lighter, more refreshing brew for the (relatively) warmer months. Truly there is a British beer for every occasion.

bitter

Bitter is the classic style of English ale. There are many definitions of this style, and they all overlap in various areas, but a classic English bitter can be anything from 3.5%abv to 4.5%abv in strength, anything from golden to brown in color, and with a classic balance of malt sweetness and hop bitterness. These beers are generally light- to medium-bodied; the key word here is drinkability. These are classic "session" beers—tasty but lower-strength beers that you can have a few of without becoming unpleasantly drunk. They are the backbone of English pub culture, something that is justifiably celebrated the world over.

Traditional English pub in summer

🏴 Harvey's Sussex Best

Head brewer and all-round good chap Miles Jenner brews a huge variety of beers at the Harvey's Brewery in Lewes, Sussex. This fabulous, pale coppery ale has a nutty but delicate toasted grain core, overlaid with gently bitter hops. A masterpiece of restraint and exceptionally drinkable.

Food match: the English classic—fish and chips

Country: England

ABV: 4%; Serving temp.: 50–55°

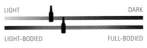

LIGHT		DARK
LIGHT-BODIED		FULL-BODIED

🏴 Coniston Bluebird Bitter

This pale copper-gold beer is a great example of the delicacy of pale golden English ales. There is a lovely cracker (think English biscuits) aroma, and a faint suggestion of floral hops. A spritz of citrus mid-palate and a dry, faintly floral finish. Dry, delicate, and very drinkable.

Country: England

ABV: 4.2%; Serving temp.: 50–55°

LIGHT		DARK
LIGHT-BODIED		FULL-BODIED

🏴 Coniston Bluebird XB

"Familiar, but different" is the tagline on this hop-enhanced version of the classic Bluebird Bitter. The familiar nutty cracker malt aroma also carries a burst of citrusy hop. The palate is tarter, and the finish is given a lemony, bitter burst. English ale with a transatlantic drawl.

Country: England

ABV: 4.4%; Serving temp.: 50–55°

LIGHT		DARK
LIGHT-BODIED		FULL-BODIED

🏴 Hall & Woodhouse Badger First Gold

Hall & Woodhouse produce a large range of Badger beers, some flavored with exotic ingredients. I prefer the ones that taste of beer. First Gold hops lend a lovely floral note to the nose and a spicy bitter orange character to this copper-colored ale. Nice fruity finish.

Country: England

ABV: 4%; Serving temp.: 50–55°

LIGHT		DARK
LIGHT-BODIED		FULL-BODIED

🏴 Shepherd Neame Spitfire

This copper-colored ale from Britain's oldest brewery has a fantastic, balanced drinkability to it. There is a note of spicy hop on the nose, alongside a lovely toasted malt aroma. The finish is hop-driven, with a dry bitterness building after the swallow.

Country: England

ABV: 4.5%; Serving temp.: 50–55°

LIGHT		DARK
LIGHT-BODIED		FULL-BODIED

🏴 Wylam Angel

Celebrating 10 years of Antony Gormley's colossal sculpture, The Angel of the North, in northeast England, this beer's copper color mirrors the rusty patina of the sculpture. Sweet toffeeish malt (all of Wylam's beers have an enjoyable touch of sweetness) and plenty of zesty citrus fruitiness. Very drinkable.

Food match: somewhat incongruously, chicken teriyaki skewers or pork satay
Country: England
ABV: 4.3%; Serving temp.: 50–55°

LIGHT ——————— DARK
LIGHT-BODIED ——————— FULL-BODIED

🇺🇸 Goose Island Honkers Ale

Drawing inspiration from classic English ale, this mid-brown ale has a lovely caramel malt aroma and a nicely rounded, almost restrained hoppiness. The rounded, mouth-filling flavor is predominantly nutty malt, with plenty of bittering hop, but not much in the way of aroma hop.
Country: USA
ABV: 4.3%; Serving temp.: 50–55°

LIGHT ——————— DARK
LIGHT-BODIED ——————— FULL-BODIED

🏴 Wolf Best Bitter

This classic copper-colored English ale has kept abreast with the transatlantic interbreeding of the last decade. A big, citrus hop aroma mingles nicely with toasted grain maltiness. There's a little toasted grain mid-palate and a nutty finish with some hop zest.
Country: England
ABV: 3.9%; Serving temp.: 50–55°

LIGHT ——————— DARK
LIGHT-BODIED ——————— FULL-BODIED

🇺🇸 Black Diamond Amber Ale

"British Inspired, American Brewed" states the label of this copper-amber beer. The aroma has a gentle citrus quality (orange, grapefruit) over a gentle toffee malt note. Medium-dry palate, with some toasted grain husk coming to the fore after the swallow. Dry, grapefruity finish.
Country: USA
ABV: 4.5%; Serving temp.: 50–55°

LIGHT ——————— DARK
LIGHT-BODIED ——————— FULL-BODIED

🏴 Woodforde's Wherry

Good English ale delivers bags of flavor at modest strengths. This is a great example, from the citrus zest on the nose to the sherbety burst of resinous hops on the tongue, through to a finish that keeps citrus hops and toasted malt in perfect balance.
Country: England
ABV: 3.8%; Serving temp.: 50–55°

LIGHT ——————— DARK
LIGHT-BODIED ——————— FULL-BODIED

Angel of the North, monument welcoming travelers to the north-east of England

English pub inside the vaults under Charing Cross station, London

🏴 Batemans XXXB

There is a mouthwatering fruitiness to the aroma of this beer, with an undercurrent of toffee. A little butterscotch character shows mid-palate, which has a touch of sweetness, and the finish develops a pleasant nutty bitterness. Nicely balanced, a textbook example of an English ale.

Food match: the nutty malt matches perfectly with roast turkey and cranberry sauce
Country: England
ABV: 4.8%; Serving temp.: 50-55º

🏴 Marston's Pedigree

Pedigree is one of those beers that seems simple but has a lot going on. From the slight whiff of sulfur (Burton water is high in sulfates), to the crunchy crystal malt backbone, to the dab of butterscotch mid-palate, to the nutty and bittersweet finish, this is an unreconstructed British classic.
Country: England
ABV: 4.5%; Serving temp.: 50-55º

🏴 Wadworth 6X

Nut brown, with some muted hop aromas and a nice dab of butterscotch sweetening everything up. On the palate, medium-sweet maltiness gives way to a fairly dry, hoppy finish, with hints of nut and toffee. A classic English ale, but still holding its own.
Country: England
ABV: 4.3%; Serving temp.: 50-55º

🏴 Hook Norton Old Hooky

For such a modestly strong ale, there is a lot of complexity here. Toasted grain husk, toffee, bags of fruit character (plums, dried fruit), and a dab of butterscotch on the nose, followed by a palate full of fruit, nuts, and spice, and a bittersweet finish.
Country: England
ABV: 4.6%; Serving temp.: 50-55º

🏴 Brakspear Bitter

When the original Brakspear brewery was sold, the purchasers used and rebuilt as much of the plant as possible. The beers are consistently good, as this copper-brown ale shows. Toasted malt and toffee on the nose, light and crisply bitter on the palate. A classic English session ale.
Country: England
ABV: 3.4%; Serving temp.: 53-55º

⊞ Timothy Taylor Landlord

Taylor's Landlord is unjustly famous for being Madonna's favorite English ale. I say unjustly, as it's a damn fine beer even without a celebrity endorsement. Amber-gold, with a lovely aroma of hops (orange, tangerine) and some caramel. Medium-bodied, with amazing balance and zesty drinkability. A classic.

Food match: in the absence of crispy chicken skin, sliced cold chicken on salad greens, with an orange dressing
Country: England
ABV: 4.3%; Serving temp.: 52–58°

⊞ Black Sheep Black Sheep Ale

One of the classic no-nonsense Yorkshire ales, the copper-colored Black Sheep is a modest delight. Toffee, caramel, and butterscotch on the nose are supported by a pithy hopsack aroma. The beer is fairly dry in the mouth, and the gentle dry bitterness builds in the finish.
Country: England
ABV: 4.4%; Serving temp.: 55°

🏴 Felinfoel Double Dragon

Felinfoel is celebrated mostly for being the first European brewer to put beer in cans—a shame, as this coppery beer is rather good. There is a touch of ripe apple alongside the toffee and nut aroma, a balance to the palate, and dry nuttiness in the finish.
Country: Wales
ABV: 4.2%; Serving temp.: 50–55°

⊞ Acorn Barnsley Bitter

Named after its hometown, this beer was once so popular that when production ceased in the 1960s, people took to the streets to protest. This reincarnation has a robustly nutty aroma brightened with some hop spice; a full, dry palate; and an intensity well beyond its modest strength.
Country: England
ABV: 3.8%; Serving temp.: 50–55°

⊞ Hogs Back Traditional English Ale (TEA)

There are pleasant fruity esters on the nose (banana, bubblegum) and orange notes from the hops. Sweetish in the mouth, with some toffee and more bitter orange, and a rounded finish that starts sweet and grows softly bitter.
Country: England
ABV: 4.2%; Serving temp.: 50–55°

Stunning view of Ilkley Moor, Yorkshire, near Keighley where Timothy Taylor is brewed

brown ale

Brown ale is a sub-style of English ale. Traditionally, it has differed from other styles of English ale by being less hop-accented, although that is not to say that there is no hop character. But it is hard to be definitive about it, as some examples are a little sweeter, others drier, and some almost austere. And to rely on the English classic (Newcastle Brown Ale) to define the style would be a mistake—American craft brewers have taken the rounded nuttiness of the original and run with it, adding aroma hops and thereby infuriating purists. As ever, both the old school and the new wave have their merits.

Sacks of malt used for making brown ale

⊞ Samuel Smith's Nut Brown Ale

As you would expect from the name, there is a lovely malt-driven nuttiness to this copper-brown ale. Dried fruit and toasted malt on the nose lead to a silky sweet palate, with more nutty malt. Hops make a late appearance after the swallow. A classic example.

Food match: broiled meats or sweeter hard cheeses—Muenster or Gouda are great
Country: England
ABV: 5%; Serving temp.: 55°

▤ Dogfish Head Indian Brown Ale

A massive aroma of roasted barley comes bursting from this dark ruddy-brown beer, with some restrained leafy hop notes detectable. Coffee and chocolate are evident in the aroma and on the silky-textured palate. Dried fruit and nutty chocolate dominate the finish. Delicious.
Country: USA
ABV: 7.7%; Serving temp.: 50–55°

▤ Shmaltz He'Brew Messiah Bold

Pouring a very dark brown, this beer has tons of lovely roast malt aroma—toffee, scorched brown sugar, a hint of smoke, and some citrusy hop. The palate is big and sweetish, becoming drier and more bitter after the swallow, with dried fruit notes developing.
Country: USA
ABV: 5.6%; Serving temp.: 50–55°

▤ Brooklyn Brown Ale

Perhaps in the belief that bigger equals better, there is a surprising amount of hops in this brown ale. The aroma is perfumed and citrusy, with some coffee and cola notes in the background. The finish is aromatic and hoppy, with chocolate and coffee emerging.
Country: USA
ABV: 5.6%; Serving temp.: 50–54°

⊞ Scottish & Newcastle Newcastle Brown

Sold, relocated, and now brewed by the tanker-load, Newkie Brown is not what it once was. But there is enough of the original left to give an idea of what brown ale should be—nutty, toffeeish, with a rounded finish.
Country: England
ABV: 4.7%; Serving temp.: 50°

extra special bitter

There's an argument that ESB isn't really a style of beer but refers specifically to Fuller's ESB (Extra Special Bitter), and all others are interpretations of it. As a style (if style it is), it tends to be between 5%abv and 6%abv and has both a sweet malty edge and a bright, spicy hop profile. It's really too strong for consumption in any quantity, but great with food (steak and onions would be a good match). The Sixpoint Brownstone is a brown ale carried over from the previous section—sampled from tank at the brewery, it was exceptionally good.

Sizzling steak and onions make a delicious accompaniment to ESB.

🏴󠁧󠁢󠁥󠁮󠁧󠁿 Fuller's ESB

Arguably the Extra Special Bitter (ESB) against which all others are measured, there is a lovely aroma of toffee, gingerbread, and hop spice to this coppery beer. The palate is like a slice of gingerbread with toffee sauce, with plenty of orangey bitterness developing in the medium-dry, spicy finish.

Food match: a cheeseburger with the works (proper cheese, not processed slices)
Country: England
ABV: 5.9%; Serving temp.: 50–55°

LIGHT ——————————— DARK
LIGHT-BODIED ——————— FULL-BODIED

🇺🇸 Sixpoint Brownstone

There is a surprisingly sweet intensity to this dark brown ale, although it somehow manages to escape being cloying. Caramel, toffee, and toasted malt all pervade the aroma, and the medium-sweet palate carries a nicely creamy, roasted bitterness.
Country: USA
ABV: 5.8%; Serving temp.: 48–52°

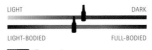

LIGHT ——————————— DARK
LIGHT-BODIED ——————— FULL-BODIED

🇺🇸 Speakeasy Prohibition Ale

This amber-brown beer has a heady aroma full of toffee, scorched sugar, and fresh hops, capturing their resinous quality as though rubbed in the hand. Sticky hops slew across the palate like a jackknifed truck on a freeway. Naughty but nice.
Country: USA
ABV: 6.1%; Serving temp.: 45–50°

LIGHT ——————————— DARK
LIGHT-BODIED ——————— FULL-BODIED

✚ Robinson's Double Hop

Sitting broadly in the ESB style, Double Hop is a pale copper-colored beer with a wonderfully pithy, resinous hop aroma (bitter orange, hopsack). The relatively weighty mouthfeel (nice caramel malt) is carried along well with a spicy hop punchiness. Finish is bittersweet—toffee, orange pith.
Country: England
ABV: 5%; Serving temp.: 50–55°

LIGHT ——————————— DARK
LIGHT-BODIED ——————— FULL-BODIED

🇺🇸 Rogue Brutal Bitter

This ESB-style ale has a very spicy hop aroma, with a high dose of the same on the palate. Malt lends body, but really in a supporting role. Spicy, dry, and very drinkable, like an English ale crossed with an American IPA. It's not really brutal, but it does scuff the tastebuds up a little.
Country: USA
ABV: 6.2%; Serving temp.: 53–57°

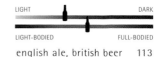

LIGHT ——————————— DARK
LIGHT-BODIED ——————— FULL-BODIED

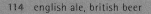 Grand Teton Bitch Creek ESB

The dark ruddy-brown of this beer suggests a forceful malt character, which is evident on the nose. There's toffee and caramel alongside a hearty, resinous hop character. Caramel and bruised-apple flavors mid-palate are gradually overlaid with bitterness. Down-to-earth, punchy, and robust.

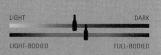

Food match: anything that will take a side order of caramelized onions
Country: USA
ABV: 5.5%; Serving temp.: 46-48°

LIGHT — DARK
LIGHT-BODIED — FULL-BODIED

✚ Bateman Victory Ale

Brewed to celebrate the late George Bateman's buyout of the brewery, Victory Ale is a real treat. This medium-dark ale has an ESB character—fruity malt and spicy hops on the nose and an initial assertive attack of sweet malt, followed by a good sweeping finish of spicy hops.
Country: England
ABV: 6%; Serving temp.: 50-55°

LIGHT — DARK
LIGHT-BODIED — FULL-BODIED

🏴 Brains Dark

This beer is starting to be recognized as a minor classic. Lovely dark roast malts lend an aroma of chocolate, coffee, and licorice, while the palate has a lovely soft, creamy quality. Low hop bitterness and a silky-sweet finish. Splendidly flavor-packed for a weaker beer.
Country: Wales
ABV: 3.9%; Serving temp.: 50-55°

LIGHT — DARK
LIGHT-BODIED — FULL-BODIED

✚ Panimoravintola Huvila ESB

ESB is ale with more everything—hops, malt, flavor, and alcohol. This is a good example—bright orange in color, with a robust hop presence (developing spicy aromas), nice juicy fruit, and a medium finish that has caramel and resinous hop characters.
Country: Finland
ABV: 5.2%; Serving temp.: 50-55°

LIGHT — DARK
LIGHT-BODIED — FULL-BODIED

✚ Holden's Black Country Mild

A dark brown mild with an aroma of dried fruit, nuts, licorice, and a hint of smoke. The smoke briefly comes to the fore on the palate, before fading into the softly fruity palate, which has a hint of port wine and a slightly savory quality. Finishes light and dry.
Country: England
ABV: 3.7%; Serving temp.: 53-57°

LIGHT — DARK
LIGHT-BODIED — FULL-BODIED

Savolinna Castle near Saimaa in Finland, where Panimoravintola Huvila is brewed

mild

There's a widespread misunderstanding that "mild" is synonymous with "weak" in the beer lexicon. It's true that mild does tend to be lower in alcohol, but the term specifically refers to reduced hop rate, producing a milder, less bitter beer. Reduced hopping allows the fruitiness of the malt in the beer to come to the fore. The milds listed here (and on the previous page) are fairly typical of the style—lower alcohol, fairly dark in color, with a slight tendency to sweetness. They are beers that have a particularly nourishing and restorative quality to them.

The Great British Beer Festival, held annually since 1975, has been a huge boost to the industry

🏴 Moorhouse's Black Cat

This dark brown ale with ruby highlights has a lovely aroma of coffee, chocolate, and fresh tobacco. Despite being relatively low in alcohol, a lot of flavor is packed in here—coffee, bitter chocolate, and a suggestion of brandy barrels. The roasted, nutty, smoky finish is very enjoyable.

Food match: the contrast of flavors and textures makes this a surprisingly great match for risotto

Country: England
ABV: 3.4%; Serving temp.: 48-52°

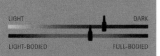

🏴 Leeds Midnight Bell

With the historic Tetley's Brewery set to close in 2011, it's up to this new Leeds-based micro to carry on the town's brewing tradition. With its dark chestnut color, rich dark fruitiness, and smooth, nutty, dark chocolate finish, it looks more than capable of doing so.

Country: England
ABV: 4.8%; Serving temp.: 50-55°

🏴 Rudgate Ruby Mild

Despite its tiny capacity and modest surroundings (an old airfield, now an industrial park), Rudgate turns out some cracking ales, and this ruby mild is clearly one of the best. Nutty malt on the nose, a bittersweet roasted palate, and a nutty coffee-toned dryness to the finish.

Country: England
ABV: 4.4%; Serving temp.: 52-56°

🏴 Greene King XX Mild

This is a lesser-known beer from a large producer, which manages to be everything a mild should be. Very dark brown, full-bodied, soft and sweet on the palate, with nutty roasted malt character, coffee, and chocolate. Dried fruit and a hint of tartness in the dry finish.

Country: England
ABV: 3%; Serving temp.: 51-55°

🏴 Cropton Balmy Mild

There is a complexity about the aroma that is hard to pin down, until you realize that there is a touch of hop. In a mild? OK, we'll let that go. A dry, malty body with a touch of roasted chicory and nuts about it, and a nutty, hoppy finish. It shouldn't work, but it does.

Country: England
ABV: 4.4%; Serving temp.: 52-56°

pale golden ale

Pale golden ale is a relatively new style to the British brewing tradition. Until a watershed moment in the late 1980s, ale was mostly to be found in any color as long as it was brown. The two pioneering beers that changed all that were Exmoor Ales Exmoor Gold and Hop Back Summer Lightning. Both were brewed using only pale malt, and crisply hopped to accentuate their light, summery nature. Both were an instant success, giving ale drinkers something lighter and fresher to drink during the warmer months. I find it very exciting to think that everything in this section can be traced back to just two beers.

Quality control is an essential part of the brewing process

 Exmoor Ales Exmoor Gold

Along with Hop Back Summer Lightning, this pale beer helped redefine real ale when it was launched, it being one of the first pale golden ales. It's still a beauty—softly floral and slightly grassy, with a sweet pale malt core and a hint of citrus zest in the finish.

Food match: broiled chicken wings with spicy dipping sauce
Country: England
ABV: 4.5%; Serving temp.: 48-53°

LIGHT ▮ DARK
LIGHT-BODIED ▮ FULL-BODIED

 Durham Cloister

There is a lovely robust quality to the Durham Brewery's beers, demonstrating brewer Steve Gibbs's devotion to his craft. Even this lighter golden ale packs a flavor punch—zesty Cascade hops on the nose; a firm, sweet malt core to the palate; and a burst of grapefruit in the finish.
Country: England
ABV: 4.5%; Serving temp.: 48-53°

LIGHT ▮ DARK
LIGHT-BODIED ▮ FULL-BODIED

Wolf Golden Jackal

Pale golden English ale is a great style for summer quaffing, and this example pushes all the right buttons. Lemon sherbet sets the tongue tingling, pale stone fruit slips languorously across the palate, and a burst of floral zest bids a brief goodbye, until the next mouthful. Really jolly good.
Country: England
ABV: 4%; Serving temp.: 48-53°

LIGHT ▮ DARK
LIGHT-BODIED ▮ FULL-BODIED

✖ Cairngorm Trade Winds

This burnished golden beer is a multi-award winner. The use of elderflower as a flavoring gives a perfumed lift to the nose, alongside citrus hops. A rounded bitterness emerges on the palate, and the perfumed floral note re-emerges in the gently bitter finish.
Country: Scotland
ABV: 4.3%; Serving temp.: 48-53°

LIGHT ▮ DARK
LIGHT-BODIED ▮ FULL-BODIED

 Brains SA Gold

This pale golden beer bursts onto the palate with a sappy sweetness, some tropical fruit character, and a little creaminess mid-palate, and leaves a lightly bitter finish with hints of toasted grain. A textbook pale golden English ale, but for the fact that it's brewed in Wales.
Country: Wales
ABV: 4.7%; Serving temp.: 48-53°

LIGHT ▮ DARK
LIGHT-BODIED ▮ FULL-BODIED

 Hop Back Summer Lightning

One of the first-ever pale golden ales, a style that is now prevalent in the UK. Brewer John Gilbert created an instant classic in the microbrewery behind the Wyndham Arms pub in Salisbury, Wiltshire. Pale malt and softly citrus hops dominate, with a gentle spiciness (coriander seed, lemongrass) in the finish.

Food match: Thai fishcakes or corn patties with chile dipping sauce
Country: England
ABV: 5%; Serving temp.: 48–53°

LIGHT — DARK
LIGHT-BODIED — FULL-BODIED

Moorhouse's Pendle Witches Brew

The use of torrefied (highly heated) wheat gives a distinct nutty, grain-husk aroma to this copper-gold beer. There is a lovely interplay of bittersweetness on the palate, with some zesty, citrusy hop character appearing mid-palate. A nutty dryness emerges in the finish.
Country: England
ABV: 5.1%; Serving temp.: 48–53°

LIGHT — DARK
LIGHT-BODIED — FULL-BODIED

Springhead Roaring Meg

There's a soft lemon character to this beer, supported by a hint of Eastern spicing (lemongrass? coriander?) that confers an easy drinkability beyond its strength. A pale malt backbone supports throughout, allowing zesty hops to shine through in the finish.
Country: England
ABV: 5.5%; Serving temp.: 48–53°

LIGHT — DARK
LIGHT-BODIED — FULL-BODIED

Otley O-Ho-Ho

The sleek, minimal branding of these beers is a talking point in itself, and happily the beers don't disappoint. A punchy fruit aroma (lemon, apricot), a big mouth-filling burst of sweet pale malt, followed by a twist of bitter lemon zest. Finishes dry, with a faint smoky quality.
Country: Wales
ABV: 5%; Serving temp.: 48–53°

LIGHT — DARK
LIGHT-BODIED — FULL-BODIED

Sharp's Chalky's Bite

Chalky's Bite was devised by Sharp's head brewer in collaboration with UK seafood chef Rick Stein. Matured for three months over fennel seed, this pale but full-bodied beer has a sappy sweetness at its core and a soft malty finish that displays an anise note.
Country: England
ABV: 6.8%; Serving temp.: 48–53°

LIGHT — DARK
LIGHT-BODIED — FULL-BODIED

Traditional English morris dancers at a hop festival in Faversham, Kent

Until 2006, some Young's (now Wells & Young's) beers were delivered by a horse-drawn dray

🏴 Thornbridge Kipling

Not many small breweries employ more than one brewer; Thornbridge currently employs four. This "South Pacific Pale Ale" showcases the unique fruity delicacy of the Nelson Sauvin hop—gently aromatic, softly textured, and redolent of lychees, vanilla, and passion fruit.

Food match: spiced almonds, Thai-spiced fish
Country: England
ABV: 5.2%; Serving temp.: 48–52°

🇦🇺 Cooper's Sparkling Ale

It's clear that there is more than a passing nod to the English ale tradition in this Aussie brew. The pale crunchy malt core supports a pear and soft apple flavor, with perhaps a touch of banana hiding in the wings. The finish is clean and crisp.
Country: Australia
ABV: 5.8%; Serving temp.: 50°

🇦🇺 Cooper's Pale Ale

This is one of those brews that pricks the interest of the beer-curious into discovering the world of good beer. A light, grainy note hints at a lager, but this pale ale is top-fermented and bottle-conditioned. Pears and bubblegum mingle with a light bitterness in the finish.
Country: Australia
ABV: 4.5%; Serving temp.: 46–53°

🏴 Wells & Youngs Young's Kew Gold

Although now relocated from London and merged with Charles Wells to form Wells & Young's, the beers are still good (although, predictably, not what they once were). This delicate golden beer has a light malty aroma, nice citrus tones mid-palate, and a grassy hop finish. A good summer quaffer.
Country: England
ABV: 4.8%; Serving temp.: 48–52°

🏴󠁧󠁢󠁳󠁣󠁴󠁿 Isle Of Skye Hebridean Gold

There's a perfume to the aroma of this delicate ale that brings to mind heather honey, though the "secret" ingredient is actually porridge oats, detectable in the soft texture and faintly toasted aftertaste. Light, dry, and slightly tart, this is a great apéritif beer.
Country: Scotland
ABV: 4.3%; Serving temp.: 48–53°

well-hopped "session" beers

When the sun is out and the temperature rises (which does occasionally happen in the UK), pale golden ales become things of great beauty. The beers in the following section are perfect all-rounders—a quick one after work, before dinner, or at the end of a long walk in the countryside. The slightly lower alcohol levels are a bonus, but what really makes the majority of these beers stand out is their bright, zesty hop presence. There is little emphasis on malt character, with pale malt acting as a blank canvas onto which the hop character is projected.

A Scottish brewery on the banks of the Clyde in Glasgow

⚔ Harviestoun Bitter & Twisted

This zesty pale bitter was part of the new wave of Scottish craft brewing, and brewer Stuart Cail has created an instant classic. Burnished gold in color, with a mouthwatering citrus aroma (lemon and grapefruit), a textbook interplay of bitter and sweet on the palate, and a more bitter grapefruit flavor in the finish.

Food match: broiled chicken (or a more robust fish) in a lemon–lime marinade
Country: Scotland
ABV: 4.2%; Serving temp.: 48–54°

✚ St Austell Tribute

I'm always skeptical of beers that claim to capture the essence of a place. Is the essence of Cornwall really pale malt and grapefruit zest? On the other hand, drinking Tribute clearly evokes the fresh Atlantic Ocean sluicing across a rocky coastal outcrop. Fresh, zesty, dry, and very drinkable.
Country: England
ABV: 4.2%; Serving temp.: 50–54°

✚ Daleside Blonde

Describing itself as a "lagered ale," this golden beer has an aroma of toasted grain husk with a twist of lemon. The slight sweetness to the palate is balanced with zesty, lemony hops. The finish is dryish, with a burst of lemon sherbet. A Yorkshire kölsch, perhaps?
Country: England
ABV: 4.3%; Serving temp.: 46–50°

✚ Elland Beyond The Pale

Beyond the pale, but not by much, this burnished golden ale has an alluring citrus aroma with a slightly heady, perfumed tropical fruit note. Full-bodied, with more tropical fruit, finishing with a soft, medium-dry bitterness.
Country: England
ABV: 4.2%; Serving temp.: 52–55°

✚ Outlaw Wild Mule

Medium-pale gold, with an appetizing tropical fruit aroma (passion fruit, gooseberry). Great hop attack on entrance (more gooseberry), with an intense bitterness that fades to a gentle bitter dryness. More passion fruit in the finish, alongside a nutty, toasted pale malt flavor.
Country: England
ABV: 3.9%; Serving temp.: 50–54°

english ale, british beer 125

⊞ Dark Star Hophead

Pale straw-gold, with zesty aromas (grapefruit, tangerine) that simultaneously make my mouth water and my throat dry. Punchy hop attack (citrus zest), with some soft spice notes (coriander) and a burst of passion fruit on the swallow. Bitterness builds gently in the finish.

Food match: none needed, but lightly spiced nuts or chickpeas would be good
Country: England
ABV: 3.8%; Serving temp.: 48–53°

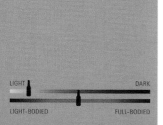

⊠ BrewDog Trashy Blonde

Although known for its uncompromising attitude and extreme beers, BrewDog makes some great "ordinary" beers too. Trashy Blonde is a golden ale with a lovely tropical fruit nose (passion fruit, mango), a sweetish palate (more mango), and a long, softly bitter finish.
Country: Scotland
ABV: 4.1%; Serving temp.: 48–53°

⊞ Roosters YPA

Pale straw-gold in color, with a heady floral note (violets, perhaps?) and a soft red berry character. There is an underlying tropical fruit character (passion fruit, guava) woven into the clean, toasty pale palate. The finish is dry and fresh, with the same floral note reappearing.
Country: England
ABV: 4.3%; Serving temp.: 48–53°

⊞ Crouch Vale Brewer's Gold

Slightly more full-bodied and fruity than most golden ales, this has an enticing aroma of tropical fruit and citrus zest on the nose. There is a little pine resin on the palate, with more fruit notes (passion fruit), though it remains pretty dry throughout. The "Extra" version is all that, and then some.
Country: England
ABV: 4%; Serving temp.: 48–53°

⊞ Oakham JHB

Pale and golden, with a fresh, punchy aroma of citrus (lemon) and spice (lemongrass). The palate initially shows a little sweetness, but dries quickly to a medium-dry, fairly bitter finish, with a light perfumed quality— more lemons and lemongrass. A multiple award winner.
Country: England
ABV: 3.8%; Serving temp.: 48–53°

Until hop gardens were mechanized in the 1960s, growing and picking the hops provided employment for many people in parts of rural England

The Campaign for Real Ale lobbies against pressurized keg beer (pictured here), which is often filtered and pasteurized; they favor traditional cask ale.

 Copper Dragon Golden Pippin

Recent investment at this North Yorkshire micro seems set to propel it into the big time, and this pale golden beer looks to be its ace. Soft, pale malt dominates throughout, with a little hoppy zest on the nose and palate. Medium-dry finish, with some nutty pale malt.

Food match: bar snacks (nuts, pretzels), but nothing too robust or spicy
Country: England
ABV: 3.9%; Serving temp.: 48-53°

Purple Moose Snowdonia Ale

Copper-gold in color, this has a really zippy citrus aroma (orange and tangerine). The palate starts out with the same citrus burst as the aroma and is medium-sweet, with a faint phenolic note. A big burst of floral hops on the swallow, before a crisp citrus finish.
Country: Wales
ABV: 3.6%; Serving temp.: 48-53°

Sharp's Cornish Coaster

While Sharp's seems set to make its mark with Doom Bar bitter, it is the pale golden ale that does it for me. A pale malt nose with some vanilla aroma, a light clean body, and a soft lemony twist in the finish. A contemporary low-strength English ale.
Country: England
ABV: 3.6%; Serving temp.: 48-53°

Atlas Latitude Highland Pilsner

While the "pilsner" designation may be confusing here, there is a lot to like in this golden ale. The pine-needle aroma, the brisk, citrus crispness of the palate, and the persistent hop character in the finish (pine, tangerine) add up to a great little beer.
Country: Scotland
ABV: 3.9%; Serving temp.: 48-53°

Caledonian Deuchars IPA

Supreme champion at the Great British Beer Festival 2002, this pale beer is alarmingly drinkable. There is a nice interplay of toasted grain and lemony hop aroma on the nose, while the crisp, snappy pale malt palate has a wonderful mouth-filling breadth.
Country: Scotland
ABV: 3.8%; Serving temp.: 48-53°

strong ales

It's true that on a global scale, these beers aren't really that strong, especially when you think that the strongest beer featured in this book clocks in at a whopping 27%abv. Nevertheless, these beers are served by the pint, and it doesn't take much to drink too many of them (see the entry for Badger Tanglefoot for a personal tale of woe). Conversely, once you reach the 8%abv of (for example) Sam Smith's Yorkshire Stingo, you're certainly best off limiting yourself to just one, or perhaps even sharing it. These beers also pack plenty of flavor.

Many ales are available only in casks and are served on draft, rather than bottled

✠ Durham Evensong

Based on a 1937 recipe, this rich ruby-colored ale is bursting with orange peel, melon, and ripe apple aromas; a medium-sweet nuttiness to the palate; and a hint of smoked malt in the long fruity finish. CAMRA's Champion bottled beer of Britain 2005, and rightly so.

Food match: the sweet smokiness matches up well to barbecued pork ribs or smoked chicken salad
Country: England
ABV: 5%; Serving temp.: 50–55°

🇺🇸 Rogue Morimoto Black Obi Soba Ale

A very dark red ale, with a fairly persistent cream-colored head. Typically for a dark beer, coffee and dried fruit show on the nose, but also a hint of black currant, which is more obvious on the palate. The finish is surprisingly light and fruity. Very enjoyable and surprisingly complex.
Country: USA
ABV: 5%; Serving temp.: 48–52°

✠ Wychwood Hobgoblin

The Wychwood beers (and many of the beers the brewery contract-brews for others) have a fabulously juicy quality to them, and this, the flagship beer, is no exception. Dried fruit (dates) and bubblegum on the nose, a medium-sweet fruitcake palate, and a nutty, bitter finish.
Country: England
ABV: 5.2%; Serving temp.: 50–55°

▮▮ Coreff Ambrée

Listing this as an English ale will do nothing for the entente cordiale, but *tant pis.* It's full-bodied, dark brown, and sweetly malty, with a nuttiness reminiscent of an English mild. There is a hint of tart wild yeast fermentation, adding an unusual but enjoyably complex edge.
Country: France
ABV: 5%; Serving temp.: 48–52°

✠ Wells & Youngs Bombardier

The self-styled "Drink of England" is a straight-down-the-line, no-messing-with sort of a pint. Dark coppery brown, with a spicy, almost peppery hop nose, and a hint of malt-derived toffee aroma. Some caramel mid-palate, before a balanced, bittersweet finish.
Country: England
ABV: 5.2%; Serving temp.: 50–55°

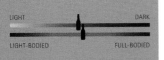 St Austell Admiral's Ale

Part of the juicy character of this bronze ale rests in Cornish Gold malt. A light toffee and orange marmalade note in the aroma sets the stage, and the palate bursts into life with a zesty citrus note (Cascade hops) and supporting crunchy malt character. Delicious, lingering, bittersweet finish.

Food match: lightly curried foods or anything that can take chutney (meat or cheese)
Country: England
ABV: 5%; Serving temp.: 48–55°

LIGHT ——————— DARK

LIGHT-BODIED ——————— FULL-BODIED

Black Sheep Riggwelter

The odd name, from old Norse, alludes to the beer's ability to land the drinker on his back, unable to right himself. Certainly a few pints of this very drinkable ale would do that. Sweet fruitcake aromas, a nutty toffee palate, and a long, faintly warming finish.
Country: England
ABV: 5.7%; Serving temp.: 50–55°

LIGHT ——————— DARK

LIGHT-BODIED ——————— FULL-BODIED

Anchor Brewing Liberty Ale

Anchor could easily lay claim to being the founding father of the American craft brewing scene, but with commendable modesty, it just concentrates on the beer. Fabulous pithy tangerine hop character over an elegant malt core. Like an English pale ale with a bit more spring in its step.
Country: USA
ABV: 5.9%; Serving temp.: 50°

LIGHT ——————— DARK

LIGHT-BODIED ——————— FULL-BODIED

Daleside Ripon Jewel

Celebrating a jeweled brooch found locally, there is a scent of orange peel and fennel seed to this amber ale. The enjoyably fruity palate (apricot? melon?) finishes on the swallow with a burst of crackerlike maltiness, before more fruit and hops weave a bittersweet finish.
Country: England
ABV: 5.8%; Serving temp.: 50–55°

LIGHT ——————— DARK

LIGHT-BODIED ——————— FULL-BODIED

Hall & Woodhouse Badger Tanglefoot

This deceptively drinkable amber-copper ale has mixed memories for me; one teenage night, I drank a gallon of it, with disastrous consequences. It's a testimony to the blend of toasted grain aromas, soft fruitiness, and slightly tart, dry finish that I can drink it again today.
Country: England
ABV: 5%; Serving temp.: 55°

LIGHT ——————— DARK

LIGHT-BODIED ——————— FULL-BODIED

Traditional pubs are still the focal point of some rural English communities

A brewery technologist pours a sample glass for testing

➕ Young's Special London Ale

There was much concern for this beer among Young's fans when the brewery merged with Charles Wells and relocated to Bedford. Fear not, the bracing, peppery quality (with a hint of eucalyptus?) of the aroma and earthy, tangy, orange-peel bitterness remain intact. Something of a classic.

Food match: will cope with most savory foods—anything from Plowman's lunch to burritos or barbecue
Country: England
ABV: 6.2%; Serving temp.: 50–55°

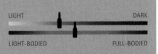

LIGHT   DARK

LIGHT-BODIED   FULL-BODIED

➕ Black Sheep Yorkshire Square Ale

Named after the slate double-decker fermentation vessel, traditional to Yorkshire, that is said to impart a more robust, rounded character to the beer. Accordingly, this has Black Sheep's hallmark toffee, butterscotch, and hopsack notes, alongside a rounded, fuller finish.
Country: England
ABV: 5%; Serving temp.: 52–58°

LIGHT   DARK

LIGHT-BODIED   FULL-BODIED

➕ Thornbridge Bracia

Some beers are so complex that you just have to abandon yourself to the ride. Heady honeyed notes float above the earthy, nutty, roasted aroma. Initially sweet, then bitter mocha with a waft of peat smoke, then more savory honey flavors. Bitter chocolate and beeswax candles to finish. Mind-boggling.
Country: England
ABV: 9%; Serving temp.: 55–60°

LIGHT   DARK

LIGHT-BODIED   FULL-BODIED

➕ Duchy Originals Organic Ale

This copper-colored ale uses organic Plumage Archer barley, some of which is grown on Prince Charles' Highgrove Estate. The beer has a wonderfully juicy malt character (orange zest, ripe apple, bubblegum), a softly spicy hop edge, and a rounded, slightly sweet finish.
Country: England
ABV: 5%; Serving temp.: 53–57°

LIGHT   DARK

LIGHT-BODIED   FULL-BODIED

➕ Duchy Originals Winter Ale

Available in the winter months, this chestnut-colored ale utilizes rye and oats alongside malted barley to give a fuller, more complex beer. Caramel, nuts, and plums on nose lead to a sweetish, darker fruit palate, given a silky texture by the oats. Slightly sweet finish, rich and fairly complex.
Country: England
ABV: 6.2%; Serving temp.: 53–57°

LIGHT   DARK

LIGHT-BODIED   FULL-BODIED

english ale, british beer   135

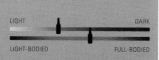 Worthington White Shield

Despite a peripatetic history, this beer is now brewed in Burton upon Trent by "unretired" brewer Steve Wellington. The burnished copper beer has notes of orange pith and blossom, black pepper, pineapple, and a big malty sweetness kept in firm check by a huge pithy hop presence. A very grown-up beer.

Food match:
strong cheese, cold roast meat, dry-cooked spiced dishes (Tandoori chicken)
Country: England
ABV: 5.6%; Serving temp.: 48–53°

LIGHT — DARK
LIGHT-BODIED — FULL-BODIED

Cooper's Vintage Ale

While this isn't the be-all-and-end-all that many make it out to be, it still has a lot going for it. Pouring a hazy copper-amber color, with dried fruit malt character on the nose. Dried fruit (dates?) also feature on the palate, with toffee and overripe fruit notes. Medium-dry finish.
Country: Australia
ABV: 7.5%; Serving temp.: 48–53°

LIGHT — DARK
LIGHT-BODIED — FULL-BODIED

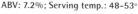 Stone Arrogant Bastard Ale

The air is filled with the bristling aroma of a million zesty, peppery hops drowning in a sea of honeyed caramel, as a wave of brown sugar, tropical fruit, and more bitter resinous hops crashes onto your palate. What did you expect from a beer with this name? Magnificently uncompromising.
Country: USA
ABV: 7.2%; Serving temp.: 48–53°

LIGHT — DARK
LIGHT-BODIED — FULL-BODIED

 Samuel Smith's Yorkshire Stingo

Fruity malt dominates the aroma, as with many of Sam Smith's ales. Dried fruit, malt loaf, brown sugar, and a rummy note point the way to a big, sweetish palate and more dried fruit (figs and dates). A tart note and a fairly dry finish keep things interesting.
Country: England
ABV: 8%; Serving temp.: 48–53°

LIGHT — DARK
LIGHT-BODIED — FULL-BODIED

 Rogue Dead Guy Ale

The brewery describes this as "in the style of a German Maibock," but if the Germans made Maibock like this, Europeans wouldn't have to import Dead Guy. Deep amber in color, with a rich toasted malt and caramel aroma. Fruity and bittersweet on the palate, with a hoppy finish.
Country: USA
ABV: 6.6%; Serving temp.: 48–53°

LIGHT — DARK
LIGHT-BODIED — FULL-BODIED

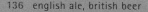

Traditional dress, and snacks such as pretzels, are part of the Oktoberfest celebrations

scottish ale

It's unlikely that putting Scottish beers in a chapter titled "English Ales, British Beers" will win me many friends north of the border, but it's true that the techniques are similar. However, there is a distinctive Scottish style of beer, and it tends to focus more on the sweetness of malt. As a consequence, they are much heartier and more robust in nature than their foppish southern cousins, even at the lower end of the strength scale. The classic, iconic "wee heavy," Orkney Skullsplitter, can be found in Chapter 12, in the Specialties section.

Sunrise on the Orkney Islands—a center of traditional Scottish craft brewing

Atlas Three Sisters

This is a modern take on the classic Scottish ale. There is a lovely upfront fruit character on the nose that seems hop-derived, with red berry fruit and a hint of ripe peach. The palate is fairly dry, with more fruit appearing in the finish alongside a faintly smoky note.

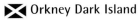

Food match: the brewery boss recommends haggis, venison, chicken, or smoked cheese
Country: Scotland
ABV: 4.2%; Serving temp.: 46-53°

Orkney Dark Island

There's an awful lot packed into this dark ale. The nose gives cocoa and freshly ground coffee, with some dried fruit. The palate is fairly dry, but an explosion of flavor on the swallow reveals smoke, fresh coffee, some nuttiness, more dark dried fruit, and some bitter hop. Very good indeed.
Country: Scotland
ABV: 4.6%; Serving temp.: 48-54°

Orkney Red MacGregor

The aroma on this copper-brown ale is splendidly complex—cherries, crushed leaves, and a faint floral note. The cherries carry through into the palate, with good toasted grain character. The finish is fairly dry, with more fruit, and the perfumed, floral note reemerging.
Country: Scotland
ABV: 4%; Serving temp.: 49-54°

Isle Of Skye Black Cuillin

I love to eat mature soft cheeses on an oatmeal cracker with a dab of honey, and the flavors here remind me of that (bar the cheese, of course). Nutty, toasted oats on the nose; some nutty coffee on the palate; and heather honey showing in the finish.
Country: Scotland
ABV: 4.5%; Serving temp.: 50-56°

McEwans Champion

Aromas of honey, banana, and dates sit alongside a faint whiff of alcohol on the nose of this amber-brown ale. Caramel and dried fruit (dates, golden raisins) fill the fairly sweet palate. The finish has a gentle whoosh of alcohol and a slightly peppery quality.
Country: Scotland
ABV: 7.3%; Serving temp.: 50-55°

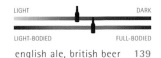

wheat beer

Wheat beer has an image problem. To most people, the notion of drinking a beer that is too cloudy to see through is anathema. It is hard to shake the feeling that there is something wrong with it, that drinking a cloudy beer will make you ill, or give you a terrible hangover. It looks dirty—it must taste awful. Of course, nothing could be further from the truth. In fact, there's a lot of hard work associated with making a beer look like that. Unlike barley, wheat doesn't have a tough outer husk, and so it has a tendency to gum up the workings of the average mash tun. And far from tasting awful, these beers are some of the softest, fluffiest, most accessible beers you could choose to drink. The cloudy wheat beers that are found on the market today are likely to be one of two types—Belgian witbier or German weissebier. Both of these translate as "white beer," although in German, weisse also indicates wheat.

The classic witbier is a cloudy orange-gold beer with a pronounced spiciness to the nose—small wonder when you realize that this style of beer is still brewed using spices, specifically Curaçao bitter orange peel and coriander seed. This style of beer was almost extinct until Pierre Celis founded the Hoegaarden Brewery in the late 1960s. Following a buyout by Interbrew (now A-B InBev), Pierre Celis moved to Austin, Texas, and started another brewery. This too was bought by a large brewery, and sadly closed. With a delicious twist of irony, his original American beer, Celis White, is now being brewed by the Belgian brewery Van Steenberge. It is a wonderfully characterful witbier, standing head and shoulders above its peers.

Bavarian weissebier is a very different beast. It is also cloudy and has a spicy edge, but using only malt, water, yeast, and hops, this spiciness is derived from fermentation rather than additions to the brew kettle. The action of yeast on the fermentable sugar is also responsible for the full, fruity esters that characterize this style of beer—banana and pear fruit; clove, nutmeg, and cinnamon spice. Hops are kept very low in the mix, serving only to add a little structure rather than to dominate the flavor—in fact, the overall bitterness is very low, making these great beers to give to people who dislike bitter beer. Then again, they are just great beers, whoever is drinking them.

So, try to set aside the prejudices of drinking cloudy beer. It's true that cloudiness isn't appropriate in most beers, but with wheat beers, it's the whole point. A tall glass of cloudy wheat beer, be it wit or weisse, is a piece of liquid gastronomy.

witbier

The beers featured in this spread are all in the Belgian style, although only the first two are classic witbiers. At their best (and although some purists may be sniffy about Hoegaarden because of its big-brewery parentage, it did win gold at the 2008 World Beer Cup), Belgian witbiers are light and refreshing. The other examples featured here are variations on a theme, mostly bumping up the body and alcohol in search of greater kicks. They are certainly bigger and fun to drink, and although they don't totally miss the point, they do lose a little of the refreshing quality of the classic style.

It's essential to angle the glass when pouring wheat beer; otherwise the fizz can result in foam pouring over the top of the glass

■■ Hoegaarden Wit

By winning the gold in its class at the World Beer Cup in 2008 (40 years after it was first brewed), Hoegaarden Wit has reasserted its credentials as the benchmark of the style. Cloudy yellow, with a citrus and spice nose, the soft, fluffy palate and short, sweetish finish give this wheat beer great drinkability.

Food match: a good all-rounder, great with a lemon-dressed seafood salad
Country: Belgium
ABV: 4.9%; Serving temp.: 48-50°

LIGHT ———————————— DARK

LIGHT-BODIED ———————— FULL-BODIED

■■ Van Steenberge Celis Wit

If this is indicative of the beer that Pierre Celis brewed when he restarted the Hoegaarden brewery in the late 1960s, then small wonder it was a hit. Bright, pungent coriander and citrus explode from the glass, spritz lightly across the palate, and leave a brisk, tangy, lemon-accented finish behind them.
Country: Belgium
ABV: 5%; Serving temp.: 48-50°

LIGHT ———————————— DARK

LIGHT-BODIED ———————— FULL-BODIED

■■ Ellezelloise Saisis

Further proof that Belgium is home to some of the world's most eccentric brewers, here's a beer that combines the peppery, herbal dryness of a tripel with the soft, aromatic spiciness of a witbier. By turns pungent, soft, tangy, and bitter; but strangely, it all hangs together very well.
Country: Belgium
ABV: 5.9%; Serving temp.: 45-50°

LIGHT ———————————— DARK

LIGHT-BODIED ———————— FULL-BODIED

■■ 't IJ Scharrel IJwit

This hazy golden beer has the 't IJ wild, savory edge, but its soft spice aroma (coriander) and rounded, fluffy texture are more reminiscent of a Belgian wheat beer. But at 7%abv, how many of these could you refresh yourself with before disaster strikes? Wheaty finish, with a lemon twist.
Country: Holland
ABV: 7%; Serving temp.: 45-50°

LIGHT ———————————— DARK

LIGHT-BODIED ———————— FULL-BODIED

■■ Abbaye Des Rocs Blanche Des Honnelles

Styling itself as a *dubbel wit*, this hazy apricot-colored beer has a bit more presence than a regular witbier. The orange-peel note to the aroma could almost be hop-derived. The soft texture carries a little more spice and some bitterness. Very nice.
Country: Belgium
ABV: 6%; Serving temp.: 45-50°

LIGHT ———————————— DARK

LIGHT-BODIED ———————— FULL-BODIED

weissebier

The wheat beers of southern Germany are classics of the beer world,
although in my experience they seem to be underappreciated. I'm
not really sure why that is. Everything that follows in the next few
pages is unquestionably delicious—soft-textured, fruity and appealing, not
overly bitter—and yet viewed with suspicion by most beer drinkers. Oh well, it's their loss.
The two non-German interlopers here aren't just included for novelty's sake—both are
serious examples of what makes a weissebier so delectably drinkable. They hold up well
under comparison with the classic examples of the style.

Obatzda (a cheese spread) drunk with wheat beer is a Bavarian delicacy

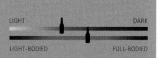 Schneider Weisse

Perhaps a little darker than usual for a hefeweisse, Schneider Weisse is a superbly drinkable example. Pouring cloudy and opaque, with a mid-brown color, there is an appealing aroma of banana bread and winter spices (cloves, allspice). Soft and spritzy, with bubblegum and more banana bread in the finish. A personal favorite.

Food match: braised pork dishes, curries, scrambled egg brunch dishes
Country: Germany
ABV: 5.4%; Serving temp.: 48–54°

LIGHT ——————————— DARK
LIGHT-BODIED ——————————— FULL-BODIED

 Bolten Ur-Weizen

There is a pleasant austerity to the beers from this brewery located a few miles west of Düsseldorf. They aren't flashy, but they are good. The Ur-Weizen has a soft yeasty aroma, with notes of bread, apples, and lemons; a soft texture; and a dryish, apple-tinged finish.
Country: Germany
ABV: 5.4%; Serving temp.: 45–50°

LIGHT ——————————— DARK
LIGHT-BODIED ——————————— FULL-BODIED

Weltenburger Kloster Hefe-Weissebier Hell

Cloudy golden yellow, with a rich, slightly creamy aroma that carries hints of honey and orange alongside the usual banana and spice notes. Fairly light-bodied, there is more spiced orange on the palate and the finish. Overall, light, clean, and very drinkable.
Country: Germany
ABV: 5.4%; Serving temp.: 46–50°

LIGHT ——————————— DARK
LIGHT-BODIED ——————————— FULL-BODIED

Erdinger Schneeweisse

Erdinger's winter brew (translated as "Snow White," sadly with no mention of any accompanying dwarfs) is a big step up in terms of excitement. Bubblegum, banana, and pears roll over a backbone of winter-spiced custard. Finish is fruity and spiced, but fairly dry.
Country: Germany
ABV: 5.6%; Serving temp.: 45–50°

LIGHT ——————————— DARK
LIGHT-BODIED ——————————— FULL-BODIED

Weihenstephaner Kristall Weissebier

This pale golden weissebier has been filtered, so it has no haze left in it. It has a soft fruitiness (ripe apples, banana), along with some cinnamon spice. Fluffy and soft on the tongue, there is another burst of fruit and spice before a medium-dry finish.
Country: Germany
ABV: 5.4%; Serving temp.: 48–54°

LIGHT ——————————— DARK
LIGHT-BODIED ——————————— FULL-BODIED

Grolsch Weizen

This is something of an oddity. It's brewed in Holland, but it has all the main attributes of a Bavarian wheat beer and a suggestion of some Belgian spicing. A cloudy apricot-color beer with bananas and cloves on the nose, deliciously creamy texture, and sweetly spiced finish. Very good indeed.

Food match: braised fennel with pork, robust fish in butter sauce
Country: Holland
ABV: 5.3%; Serving temp.: 48-52°

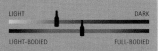

Weihenstephaner Hefe Weissebier

From the world's oldest brewery, this is (unsurprisingly) a classic example. Pale hazy orange, with clove, nutmeg, apple, and banana, and a hint of orangey hops (unusual for a weisse). The finish is medium-big, with a good persistence of fruit and spice and a faint bitterness.
Country: Germany
ABV: 5.4%; Serving temp.: 48-54°

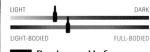

Paulaner Hefe-Weissebier

Pale orange in color, this has a nice amount of fruit on the nose (pears, ripe apples), but only a little spiciness in evidence. The palate is quite lively, with some background bitterness. There is a faintly medicinal note in the spicy, medium-dry finish.
Country: Germany
ABV: 5.5%; Serving temp.: 48-54°

Maisel's Weisse

The slightly darker color suggests that everything about Maisel's Weisse is going to be "just a little more." It's a little darker, a little fruitier, a little spicier, and a little more persistent than most of its immediate rivals. Accordingly, it's a little more interesting to drink.
Country: Germany
ABV: 5.2%; Serving temp.: 48-50°

Erdinger Weissebier

Lying under the nice fruit and spice aromas of this medium-pale weissebier, alongside an appealing floral note and a suggestion of pink bubblegum, is a hint of sweet doughy malt. The palate is soft and rounded, with a soft bready note and some spice emerging in the finish.
Country: Germany
ABV: 5.3%; Serving temp.: 46-53°

The importance of wheat in breadmaking meant that its use in beer was forbidden by German law in the sixteenth century

The Stammtisch—a table reserved for regular drinkers in German beer gardens

🇺🇸 Gordon Biersch Hefeweizen

Fully cloudy, with a gentle orange-pink peach-skin color, this has classic banana and spice hefeweizen aromas overlaid with a faint eucalyptus or mint edge. Delicious soft texture on the tongue, with some enjoyable orange notes that appear to be hop-derived, leaving a slightly dry and resinous finish.

Food match: hot spiced curries, Mexican mole, baked ham studded with cloves
Country: USA
ABV: 5.4%; Serving temp.: 48–53°

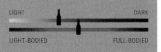

⬛ Freising Huber Weisses Original

This fairly pale golden wheat beer is hazy rather than totally cloudy, and the light lemony notes alongside the characteristic banana and spice aromas suggest an airy lightness. The palate, too, is quite light-bodied, but with a good intensity of flavor. Clean, refreshing, and very drinkable.
Country: Germany
ABV: 5.4%; Serving temp.: 48–53°

⬛ Maisel's Dunkel

A faintly smoky richness lies on top of all the more usual banana and spice aromas, combining to give the impression of fruitcake and vanilla ice cream. The silky texture of the palate enhances the illusion, and the dried fruit and winter spice notes in the finish reinforce it further.
Country: Germany
ABV: 5.2%; Serving temp.: 48–53°

⬛ Hacker-Pschorr Hefe-Weisse

Orange-gold and fully cloudy, there is an assertive —and very appealing — character to this weissebier. Banana, ripe apple, and spice aromas sit atop a hint of pink bubblegum. Full-bodied, but soft, rounded, and smooth on the palate, finishing spicy and firm.
Country: Germany
ABV: 5.5%; Serving temp.: 48–53°

⬛ Erdinger Weissebier Dunkel

This looks almost like a pint of nitrogenated stout, with its black body and fluffy white head, but that's where the similarity ends. Dried fruit on the nose, alongside ripe banana and cocoa. The palate is fuller and medium-sweet, with more dried fruit, cocoa, and cola in the medium-dry finish.
Country: Germany
ABV: 5.6%; Serving temp.: 48–53°

weissebock

We've seen the word bock before, back in the chapter on lager, and as I'm sure you remember, it indicates a stronger beer. The same rule applies here; weissebocks and weizenbocks are stronger wheat beers. There is usually a suggestion of alcohol in the flavor or the finish, but by and large, these beers are perilously drinkable, hiding their strength very well. Schönram Festweisse has ended up on this page not because it has any pretensions to being a weissebock, but with only four examples included here, the numbers need to be made up, and Festweisse is as good a contender for the job as any.

Volker Rothbauer's "Brew Owl" enables German beer drinkers to brew traditional wheat beers at home

Schneider Aventinus

The big daddy of weissebiers pours a dark mahogany brown. Banana bread and spice aromas, as well as raisins, toffee, and cocoa. Although medium-bodied, the extra strength is apparent in the intensity of the flavors—cocoa, ripe banana, winter spices. Slight warmth in the finish, with a little alcohol.

Food match: duck (with fruit sauce), pork stuffed with prunes, fruitcake
Country: Germany
ABV: 8%; Serving temp.: 48–50°

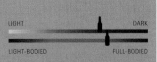

Schneider Schneider & Brooklyner Hopfen-Weisse

An innovative collaboration between the Brooklyn and Schneider breweries. Big, fruity banana esters sit atop a smooth orange hoppiness, with perfumed floral notes in the finish, alongside a slightly herbal bitterness.
Country: Germany
ABV: 8.2%; Serving temp.: 48–54°

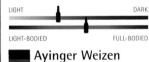

Ayinger Weizen Bock

Peachy orange in color, with a robust aroma of fruit and spice (pear, banana, clove). The beer explodes into life on the palate, full-bodied and creamy, with a lot of fruity flavor. Deliciously drinkable. A fairly new beer, and a classic in waiting.
Country: Germany
ABV: 7.1%; Serving temp.: 45–50°

Erdinger Pikantus

There is a lovely depth of dried fruit to this dark brown weissebock that nicely crowns this brewery's range. Erdinger's beers tend toward fruitiness rather than spice, and this is best displayed in the medium-sweet fig and raisin flavors found here. Dryish finish, with some warmth.

Country: Germany
ABV: 7.3%; Serving temp.: 48–55°

Schönram Festweisse

The cloudy peach-colored body of this beer throws out some classic and mouthwatering weissebier aromas—banana, clove, and some pear-drop esters. The big, fluffy-textured palate carries some clean banana flavors to the soft, rounded finish. Very nice.
Country: Germany
ABV: 5.6%; Serving temp.: 48–55°

wild & fruity

In a world concerned with sanitized food production and obsessed with "best before" dates, it's hard to know what to make of the beers in this chapter. Almost every one of them has been subject to some sort of bacterial spoilage. Now, there are some foods that are made better by the action of mold or bacteria—in fact, cheese would be a boring food, both in terms of variety and flavor, without this influence. But in beer? Really?

There are two ways that beer can be influenced by "wild" organisms. First, lambic beer is fermented with wild yeasts, and second, if the beer is aged in wood, the bacteria that live in the wood (known collectively by the term "barrel flora") also exert a powerful influence.

Lambic beer is a regional specialty of Belgium, and of Brussels in particular. The microclimate that allows wild yeasts to ferment the beer exists in only a few places. Wild yeasts are something that most conventional breweries go to great pains to avoid, but the lambic brewers of Belgium literally throw open their doors and windows to welcome them, and even go so far as to install shutters in the roof to allow the wild yeasts in. These wild, multistrain yeasts produce complex, sharp beers, with all sorts of unusual tastes and aromas. Not content with this, the brewers then age the beers for at least a year in wooden barrels, allowing the barrel flora to get to work. Lactobacillus and pediococcus bacteria and brettanomyces yeast (to name but three) all do their best to reduce a beer to a sour, spoiled mess. Beers of various ages (usually one young and one old) are blended together make a beer called gueuze, which after a secondary fermentation, emerges as an enjoyably tart beer with a pedigree that stretches back centuries. Alternatively, fruit may be added to young lambic, which not only sparks a further fermentation but also can bring a welcome note of sweetness (and a familiar flavor) to this most challenging of beer styles. But these beers aren't all overly challenging—the best show great balance, and should it all get a bit much, there is both the local specialty faro (a sweetened gueuze) or one of the more commercial, sweetened lambic beers.

A special nod must also go to the sour red (and brown) ales of Flanders, a province in the west of Belgium. These beers have long maturation on wood, and use complex multistrain yeasts to achieve a uniquely complex end product. While these beers might not be to everyone's taste, the idea that you can taste a piece of living history for just a few pounds is an exciting one.

flemish brown ale

We're entering strange territory now. The beers here are based on, or similar to, an unusual, sweet-and-sour brown ale from Flanders, with its multistrain yeast fermentation and sweet, wild complexity. Some examples also gain complexity from wood aging and the influence of organisms living in the wood. As with all Belgian (and Belgian-inspired) beers, there is a surprising amount of variation between examples, but all display the characteristic tartness to some degree. Well, except Lindeman's Pecheresse, which is a lovely little piece of fun.

The town hall in Bruges, one of the most important centers of Belgian brewing

■■ Verhaeghe Duchesse De Bourgogne

There's a slight whiff of a pickled onion jar about the aroma, an acetic twang allied to a savory, almost mineral, note. If you can summon up the courage to press on, you'll be rewarded with a superb example of a sweet-and-sharp Flemish brown ale. Complex, but very drinkable.

Food match: strong artisan cheeses, pickled herring, curried mussels

Country: Belgium
ABV: 6.2%; Serving temp.: 48–55°

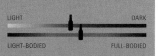

■■ Liefmans Goudenband

While this is clearly still in production (it's the base beer for Liefmans' kriek and frambozen), it seems harder to find of late. A shame, because this rich, complex brew is a classic example of Flemish brown ale, having a smooth, medium-sweet palate and a long, slightly sour finish.
Country: Belgium
ABV: 8%; Serving temp.: 55°

▤ Deschutes The Dissident

More of a lambic–brown ale hybrid, this has fruity and sour nose, and a smooth, complex cherry-accented tartness to the palate. I'm not sure there are enough superlatives to describe the complexity of this, so I'll just moan with pleasure. Mmmmm.
Country: USA
ABV: 9%; Serving temp.: 46–52°

■■ Bavik Petrus Oud Bruin

There is a malty fruitiness to the aroma of this ruddy-brown beer, alongside the characteristic complexity of a Flemish brown ale. The beer is medium-sweet in the mouth, with the finish drying slowly to leave a sweet-and-sour note and "horse blanket" brettanomyces character.
Country: Belgium
ABV: 5.5%; Serving temp.: 48–55°

■■ Riva Vondel

Pouring a ruddy brown, there is a prominent dried fruit aroma (figs) alongside some slightly musty sourness. On the palate, the beer tips toward warmth and sweetness which, although uncharacteristic for the style, is quite good fun.
Country: Belgium
ABV: 8.5%; Serving temp.: 52–58°

wild & fruity 155

 New Glarus Wisconsin Belgian Red

Not a Flemish red (like Rodenbach), nor a lambic kriek, but a distinctive and original beer. The soft pink color hints at the pound of cherries macerated for each bottle. Cherry and marzipan aromas, sweet and slightly unctuous, with a good balancing tartness to the finish. Delicious.

Food match: chocolate desserts, cheesecake, pâtés and rillettes
Country: USA
ABV: 5.1%; Serving temp.: 48–54°

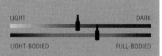

Liefmans Kriek

For me, this is the jewel in the crown of Liefmans' range. Labeled as "traditionally fermented with cherries" (and why would we doubt them?), this kriek (cherry) beer is full-flavored, with a good tart fruitiness and lovely sweet-and-sharp complexity in the finish. For stunning effect, serve with any chocolate dessert.
Country: Belgium
ABV: 6%; Serving temp.: 48–54°

Liefmans Frambozen

Following a brief halt in production and change of ownership, Liefmans' beers are now back in production. Their frambozen (raspberry) is fun but good quality. Fruity raspberry flavors layer over a slightly earthy tartness, leaving a sweet-and-sour finish.
Country: Belgium
ABV: 4.5%; Serving temp.: 48–54°

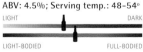

New Glarus Raspberry Tart

No doubt this beer is rated highly by connoisseurs because it is hard to find, but it's also a great beer in its own right. Opaque, purple-pink in color, with a huge raspberry bouquet. The palate is sweetly juicy, but with enough tartness to keep things enjoyable.
Country: USA
ABV: 4%; Serving temp.: 48–54°

Lindemans Pecheresse

One of Lindemans' more commercial offerings, with an eye-catching Art Deco label. Low in alcohol, this uncomplicated peach-flavored beer is ignored by beer snobs. If you just take it for what it is, a light and refreshing fruit beer, then it's perfectly enjoyable.
Country: Belgium
ABV: 2.5%; Serving temp.: 44–50°

The old brewing room (no longer in use) at the Lindemans brewery, Belgium

lambic & sour red beers

If the beers in the previous spread were firmly in strange territory, things get downright weird here. Wild yeast and wood aging comes to the fore in the dry, tart, artisanal lambic beers of Belgium and their unlikely counterparts (and, I would argue, their equals) from the United States. From the tart red beers of Rodenbach, to the spookily authentic lambics from Russian River, to the more commercial, sweetened offerings from Timmermans, these are beers that command respect. Understanding what makes them the way they are is the key to enjoying them.

Brewing Cantillon Gueuze in Brussels, Belgium

🇺🇸 Russian River Supplication (Batch 003)

There is a clear brettanomyces twang to the nose of this pale pink-brown beer, alongside lemon, cherry, and a hint of oak. Time spent in old Pinot Noir barrels imparts a fruity smoothness that is a beautiful counterpoint to the wild yeast and bacterial influence. Poised, elegant, and world-class.

Food match: great as an apéritif, or with broiled goat cheese and sharp chutney

Country: USA
ABV: 7%; Serving temp.: 48–55°

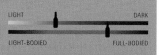

LIGHT ——————— DARK

LIGHT-BODIED ——————— FULL-BODIED

⬛⬛ Hanssens Oude Kriek

A négociant blender rather than a brewery, Hanssens buys beer from other lambic brewers and blends and ages its own gueuzes and fruit beers. This example has a splendid tartness, and although the sour cherries take some of the funkiness out, they add a zing of their own.
Country: Belgium
ABV: 6%; Serving temp.: 48–55°

LIGHT ——————— DARK

LIGHT-BODIED ——————— FULL-BODIED

⬛⬛ Rodenbach Rodenbach

Rodenbach is a blend of young and aged beers. The influence of oak and natural micro-organisms is less evident than in the Grand Cru, but this is still an enjoyably complex, softly sour beer. Excellent with bacon-wrapped broiled scallops.
Country: Belgium
ABV: 5.2%; Serving temp.: 48–55°

LIGHT ——————— DARK

LIGHT-BODIED ——————— FULL-BODIED

⬛⬛ Strubbe Crombe Oud Kriekenbier

As a natural product, this beer varies a little from batch to batch. The version sampled here had a full, pungently acetic hit to the nose (pickled onions); a zingy, woody, acidic palate; and a light cherry fruitiness coming through in the finish. Good, if you like the style.
Country: Belgium
ABV: 5.7%; Serving temp.: 48–55°

LIGHT ——————— DARK

LIGHT-BODIED ——————— FULL-BODIED

⬛⬛ Rodenbach Grand Cru

Rodenbach Grand Cru is tawny brown in color, with a wild, fusty aroma, and a hint of iron. It has a slight sweetness on the palate, but an enjoyably sharp finish. It is a textbook example of the sour red beers of western Flanders, a piece of living history, and a world classic.
Country: Belgium
ABV: 6%; Serving temp.: 48–55°

LIGHT ——————— DARK

LIGHT-BODIED ——————— FULL-BODIED

wild & fruity   159

Girardin Gueuze Black Label 1882

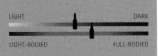

Gueuze sometimes leaves me cold, but this is a no-brainer. The mouthwatering aroma of lemons, dry sherry, and freshly sawn wood blossoms on the palate into an exceptionally complex beer —butterscotch, lemons, old cigar boxes, and brettanomyces "horse blanket." It's beer, Jim, but not as we know it.

Food match: mussels, strong cheese, pâté or rillettes with capers and sweet pickles
Country: Belgium
ABV: 5%; Serving temp.: 55°

LIGHT _____ DARK
LIGHT-BODIED _____ FULL-BODIED

Cantillon Gueuze

Some see this gueuze as the benchmark for the style, while others are perplexed by its acidity and lack of familiar beer flavors. The musty, lemon-accented nose can't fully prepare you for the shocking tartness of the palate and dry finish. The ultimate in traditional lambics, and a real "must-try."
Country: Belgium
ABV: 5%; Serving temp.: 55°

LIGHT _____ DARK
LIGHT-BODIED _____ FULL-BODIED

Russian River Beatification

Although not labeled as a gueuze, it is, and a great one too. The innocent-looking golden beer gives off intense aromas of citrus, brettanomyces character, and dusty barns. The zippy, tart palate has more citrus pith and newly chopped wood, finishing dry and pleasantly sharp.
Country: USA
ABV: 6%; Serving temp.: 46–53°

LIGHT _____ DARK
LIGHT-BODIED _____ FULL-BODIED

Oude Beersel Oude Gueuze Vieille

The key to good beer is balance. This gueuze has all the characteristic funky and abandoned cider-press aromas, alongside lemon, green apple, hay barns, and dusty old saddlebags. But there is also a softness, smoothness, and balance. A wonderfully drinkable example of the style.
Country: Belgium
ABV: 6%; Serving temp.: 50-55°

LIGHT _____ DARK
LIGHT-BODIED _____ FULL-BODIED

Boon Geuze

The pungent, acetic, brettanomyces character of this beer can certainly clear your head, and it takes a few mouthfuls to get used to the tart lemony, cidery flavor, but once your palate is fully awake, you can start to enjoy the labyrinthine complexities of this ancient style.
Country: Belgium
ABV: 6%; Serving temp.: 55°

LIGHT _____ DARK
LIGHT-BODIED _____ FULL-BODIED

Lambic beer and steamed mussels make a classic, authentically Belgian combination

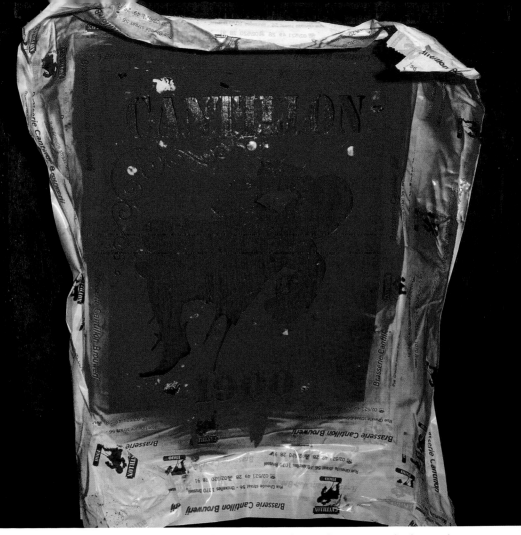

A stencil for applying the Cantillon brewery logo and name to wooden beer casks

Lindemans Gueuze Cuveé René

Cuvée René is proof of Lindemans' lambic lineage. Labeled as "Grand Cru Geuze Lambic Beer," this pale, effervescent beer has a good zippy acidity and a long, lemony finish, and stands up well to extended aging. The brewery celebrates its bicentennial in 2011; two centuries well-spent, in my opinion.

Food match: grilled goat cheese and red onion salad with lemon dressing
Country: Belgium
ABV: 5%; Serving temp.: 55°

Timmermans Gueuze Tradition

This is an interesting rendition of the style, something of a halfway house between sweetened gueuze and traditional, unsweetened examples. There's a tart green apple aroma and a slight mustiness, and although the palate starts sweet, it finishes medium-sharp and dry.
Country: Belgium
ABV: 5%; Serving temp.: 50-55°

Girardin Faro 1882

A sweetened version of Girardin's gueuze, but don't assume that means it's dumbed down. Lovely spicy aroma (nutmeg, mace, black pepper), ripe apples, and a hint of cider vinegar. The lively palate isn't sweet, but it isn't tart either. Clean finish, with more spice and overripe apples (in a good way).
Country: Belgium
ABV: 5%; Serving temp.: 45-50°

Timmermans Faro

Copper-gold in color, with an assertive aroma of toasted bread, ripe apple, and a little butterscotch. The medium-sweet palate has more toasted, nutty flavors, as well as some cloudy apple juice notes. Finish is medium-sweet, a little cloying, but with a little flick of tartness.

Country: Belgium
ABV: 4%; Serving temp.: 40-45°

Timmermans Blanche Lambicus

Lambicus is an unusually hazy lambic beer, with a dry sherry nose and a little spiciness in evidence of the palate. It's an unusual take on the style, and clearly a commercial example, but none the worse for that.

Country: Belgium
ABV: 4.5%; Serving temp.: 50-55°

non-lambic fruit beers

Of course, not all fruit beers have to be left to spoil for years in an old infected barrel, get chomped on by various yeasts and bacteria, and then blended and bottled on the third full moon of the year (or any other arcane ritual you care to invent). Some brewers believe that it's enough to ferment their beer with conventional yeasts, and just add fruit and herbs to the brew kettle. Taking the third way, Agostino Arioli of Birrificio Italiano makes deceptively simple and devilishly tasty fruit beers using alarmingly convoluted (but conventional) techniques. The results speak for themselves.

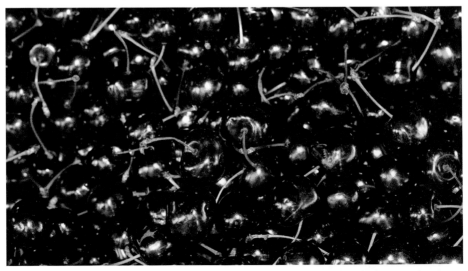

The best fruit beers are brewed using whole, unpitted fruit, not extracts or synthetic flavorings

▮▮ Birrificio Italiano Cassissona

As the name implies, this beer is flavored with a little cassis syrup, although the black currant character in this copper-gold beer is layered under peach, apricot, and melon aromas. On the palate, it's softly effervescent, with another large burst of fruit in the finish. Very good indeed.

Food match: panna cotta with fruit compote, cheesecake, broiled figs
Country: Italy
ABV: 6.5%; Serving temp.: 40–45°

LIGHT ━━━━━━━━━━ DARK
LIGHT-BODIED ━━━━━ FULL-BODIED

▮▮ Birrificio Italiano Scires

It's hard to drink a cherry beer without thinking of Belgian kriek, but this puts a new spin on the style. There is a slightly wild note to the nose, cherry candy aroma, and a touch of marzipan. The palate is dry, fruity, and tart (without being sour), and the finish is short and dry.
Country: Italy
ABV: 7.5%; Serving temp.: 40–45°

LIGHT ━━━━━━━━━━ DARK
LIGHT-BODIED ━━━━━ FULL-BODIED

✖ Williams Bros. Ebulum

This dark, ruddy ale has so much going on, it's hard to describe. The aroma has a rich roasted character, with dark fruit underlying it. The elderberries add a rich, dry red wine character to the coffee and chocolate notes in the finish. Wonderful.
Country: Scotland
ABV: 6.5%; Serving temp.: 55°

LIGHT ━━━━━━━━━━ DARK
LIGHT-BODIED ━━━━━ FULL-BODIED

✖ Williams Bros. Grozet

"Grozet" (from the Gaelic groseid) is the Scottish word for gooseberry. You can feel the tart zing of the gooseberries giving a hint of citrus to the aroma and a clean, quenching finish. Bog myrtle and meadowsweet enhance the aroma and lend a distinctive dry edge.
Country: Scotland
ABV: 5%; Serving temp.: 55°

LIGHT ━━━━━━━━━━ DARK
LIGHT-BODIED ━━━━━ FULL-BODIED

▦ Magic Hat #9

An apricot-infused beer is an unlikely candidate for glory, but a policy of broad distribution has ensured that #9 has become one of Magic Hat's best-known beers. The light fruitiness sits low in the mix, noticeable but not intrusive, and lends extra body to the finish.
Country: USA
ABV: 4.6%; Serving temp.: 45–50°

LIGHT ━━━━━━━━━━ DARK
LIGHT-BODIED ━━━━━ FULL-BODIED

wild & fruity   165

famous belgians

There's a terribly cruel joke that says it's impossible to name five famous Belgians. In fact, this joke has raised such ire that there is now a Web site, maintained by a proud Belgian, documenting no fewer than 259 famous Belgians (at the time of writing, and I'm sure that more are being added every day), with the sole intention of dispelling this myth. However, when it comes to beer, there's no question that the Belgians are famously prolific in this area. Setting aside the Trappist and abbey beers (they are covered in their own chapter), it seems as though every brewery has to produce not only a beer in a particular style, but also put its own interpretation on that style. Not only this, but this proud beer-centric nation has such a wide range of styles that it is hard to know where to stop.

I'm sure that it won't come as news that an awful lot of Belgian specialty beer is quite strong. Unlike the British and German brewing traditions, which largely adhere to the idea of using only four basic ingredients, the Belgians have a history of using cane sugar in the brew kettle as a source of fermentable material, with the ultimate aim of adding flavor and bumping up the alcohol content. It seems likely that this came about as a result of the trade in raw sugar from former Belgian colonies, although it may also be that some bright Belgian spark just realized that a couple of pounds of unrefined brown sugar added a depth of flavor and a certain oomph that is unobtainable using malt alone.

If you've ever visited Belgium, the other thing you'll know about Belgian beer (other than its ability to catch you unawares) is that each brand usually has its own special glass. From gilded chalices, to deep bulbous tulips, to unlikely round-bottomed fabrications that require a wooden stand to hold them upright, there is a seemingly endless variety of shapes, each designed to enhance one aspect or another of the beer. Having been served beers all over the world, in all manner of unlikely glassware, it still impresses me that even a relatively small Belgian bar can manage to carry a range of several dozen beers and serve them in their correct glass. Whether or not it makes a huge difference to the taste of the beer is more of a personal opinion—my opinion is that if a brewery has gone to the trouble of designing and producing a fancy glass, then why not try the beer from it? The variety is there to be savored.

So, next time someone asks you to name five famous Belgians, you can start with any of the following...

farmhouse ale & saisons

The first four beers here all loosely hang together as a group. The saisons are a splendidly complex style in their own right, have a tart, robust—nay, raucous—edge to their hoppy character, although the one English brewery eccentric enough to have a stab at this classic style could do with upping the madness quotient just a tad—maybe they need to add some cartoon gnomes into the equation? La Chouffe isn't strictly a saison, but, like so much Belgian beer, has no immediate peers, and so has ended up here. Caracole Notradamus is pretending to be a dark farmhouse ale.

Saisons were traditionally brewed in the fall and stored in the farmhouse cellar until the following harvest

Achouffe La Chouffe

What is it with the Belgians and gnomes? Urthel, the Smurfs, and Achouffe—they're all at it. Don't let it dissuade you though, because this hazy golden beer is a classic. Bursting with fruit (banana, orange) and spice (clove, nutmeg), and a sweet, toffeeish pale malt finish.

Food match: slow-cooked pork shoulder, cassoulet—classic farmhouse cooking
Country: Belgium
ABV: 8%; Serving temp.: 44-50°

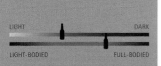

Brasserie Dupont Avec Les Bons Voeux

Originally a Christmas gift to friends of the brewery (the name means "with the best wishes of the Brasserie Dupont"), this orange beer has a snappy nose (black pepper) and medium-sweet orange and apricot flavors mid-palate before the hops kick in to a pithy finish. Very good.
Country: Belgium
ABV: 9.5%; Serving temp.: 48-54°

Dark Star Saison

A cloudy amber-gold color, with a softly spicy aroma somewhere between a German and Belgian wheat beer. The very soft mouthfeel carries a little more spiciness and fruity citrus notes. Although the bitterness is low for a saison, there is an appropriate tartness to the finish.
Country: England
ABV: 4.5%; Serving temp.: 48-54°

Brasserie Dupont Saison Dupont

Much better in a corked bottle than crown-capped, this is regarded as a classic saison. A lively copper-colored beer, which settles to a hazy orange color. Spicy hops and a complex, dry finish means that this beer is versatile with food; quality sausages are my preference.
Country: Belgium
ABV: 6.5%; Serving temp.: 48-54°

Caracole Nostradamus

Nostradamus is a rich, dark ale, with an aroma full of dried fruits and caramel. On the palate, a deep fruitcake note develops, with a pleasantly bitter note reminiscent of stewed figs. A complex spiciness persists well into the dried fruit finish.
Country: Belgium
ABV: 9%; Serving temp.: 48-54°

belgian ales

Is Belgian beer great? Yes! Is it easy to categorize? No! Palm and De Koninck are two "ordinary" Belgian ales that deserve mention, if only for being relatively easy to understand in a country that seems to pride itself on making every beer a slightly different style. De Ranke XX and Poperings Hommel are splendidly hoppy examples, not too far from being admitted to the IPA class. The Grimbergen beer could have gone in with the abbey beers in a later chapter, but given that it doesn't fall into any clearly defined style, I find myself listing it here as a strong Belgian ale.

Life is full of important choices—this Belgian beer house bears the names of the brands served inside

Palm Speciale

If you've ever visited a brewery while the mash is in progress, you'll recognize the wholesome, malty aroma of this copper-gold beer. The malt character also gives the palate a solid, mouth-filling quality. Medium-sweet, but becoming drier in the finish. Uncomplicated, but very enjoyable.

Food match: pretzels, nuts, potato chips, or garlic-rubbed toasted bread
Country: Belgium
ABV: 5.4%; Serving temp.: 54°

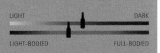

De Koninck De Koninck

For a modest domestic beer, this has a lot going for it. Pin-bright and burnished copper in color, it has an aroma of caramel and a slightly mealy (oats?), almost earthy edge. Palate is rounded and mouth-filling and, although uncomplicated, has a pleasantly wholesome, satisfying quality.
Country: Belgium
ABV: 5%; Serving temp.: 45–55°

Van Eecke Poperings Hommel

"Hommel" means "hop" in the local dialect, and it isn't too much of a stretch to classify this hazy copper-gold beer as belonging to the IPA style. The fruity, bubblegum aroma gives way to an orange hoppiness and a bittersweet finish. Excellent.
Country: Belgium
ABV: 7.5%; Serving temp.: 50°

De Ranke XX Bitter

If I had to pigeonhole this, I might describe it as a very well-hopped blonde beer, except blonde beers are never well-hopped, and this doesn't have enough malt sweetness. You see how hard Belgian beer is to describe? Wonderfully hoppy, medium-dry, with grapefruit character all the way through.
Country: Belgium
ABV: 6.2%; Serving temp.: 46–53°

Grimbergen Cuvée De L'Ermitage

Grimbergen's fancy cuvee sits stylistically between a dubbel and a quadrupel, although it lacks intensity. Soft fruit on the nose leads to a medium palate with hints of toffee, nuts, and bitter orange. Finish is dry, with smokiness, toffee, and bitterness.
Country: Belgium
ABV: 7.5%; Serving temp.: 51–56°

strong belgian ale

Almost unbelievably, these sort of hold up as a group. They are very good representatives of the kind of beers that the Belgians brew—not only do you not find them anywhere else in the world, but the rest of the world in fact regards them with a mixture of awe, fear, and suspicion. Kwak is a good beer that has become internationally known for its glass—a mini yard of ale, like a trumpet horn, with a rounded bulbous base that necessitates its own little wooden stand. Only in Belgium...

Bottle caps from the world's finest ales are prized collector's items.

Het Anker Gouden Carolus Classic

They do things right at the Het Anker Brewery. This ruddy-brown ale has a fairly restrained aroma of caramel, pepper, and toffee, but in the mouth: POW! An explosion in a dried fruit factory sends prunes, figs, and raisins soaring across the palate, followed by a licorice chaser finish.

Food match: winter fare—hearty stews, pot roasts
Country: Belgium
ABV: 8.5%; Serving temp.: 50–55°

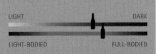

Bosteels Kwak

Famous as much for its odd-shaped glass as anything else, the strong, coppery-colored Kwak has been the downfall of many a curious beer tourist. The soft spicy aroma (gingerbread?) and smooth, sugar core hide the alcohol well, with just a slight warmth evident in the finish.
Country: Belgium
ABV: 8.4%; Serving temp.: 50–55°

Van Honsebrouck Kasteel Bruin

Big spirited aromas of butterscotch and bananas waft from this tawny monster, tipping you off that something wicked is coming your way. An explosion of sweet malt on the tongue evolves into a sweetly warming finish of fruit and marzipan. A beer to be taken seriously.
Country: Belgium
ABV: 11%; Serving temp.: 50–55°

Hoegaarden Forbidden Fruit

A deep, dark, ruddy ale, with a sweetly dark fruit aroma (plums and prunes) and a long, drying finish. The label depicts Adam and Eve before their fall from grace, each enjoying a glass of beer. Perhaps their judgment about the apple was subsequently impaired?
Country: Belgium
ABV: 8.5%; Serving temp.: 50–55°

Dubuisson Bush

There is a tell-tale note of brooding power on the nose of this little beast—sherry, and perhaps a hint of cognac too. Toffeeish malt bursts onto the palate, and then a nutlike bitterness develops. Very drinkable. Really, I'm amazed the Belgians get anything done at all.
Country: Belgium
ABV: 12%; Serving temp.: 50–55°

famous belgians   173

strong golden ale

Don't get this group confused with the British pale golden ales—most of these are twice as strong, although on the whole, equally drinkable. This last grouping of idiosyncratic brews is headed up by an undisputed world classic. Duvel is renowned for its easy drinkability, and many an unwary traveler to Belgium has been caught by downing too many of them too quickly. Despite its pale, lagerlike appearance, this is a very strong ale, usually served cold enough to hide its alcoholic character. Caveat imbiber.

Café Vlissinghe, Bruges. Dating back to 1515, this is the oldest bar in Belgium

 Moortgat Duvel

If you haven't tried Duvel yet, you need to remedy that immediately. Seriously, put the book down now and go find some. The snappy Saaz hop and schnapps aroma alone sets the mouth watering. The bittersweet interplay of pale malt and bitter hops is a delight, making the beer perilously drinkable. A true classic.

Food match: broiled or barbecued fish, with lemon and salsa verde
Country: Belgium
ABV: 8.5%; Serving temp.: 48–53°

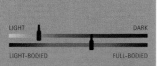

 Van Honsebrouck Kasteel Triple

The aroma of this pale beer calls to mind dry fino sherry or perhaps a hint of gueuze. The palate too has a savory, almost salty quality, with a herbal spiciness from the hops. There is a slightly medicinal note to the finish, and the alcohol is surprisingly well-hidden.
Country: Belgium
ABV: 11%; Serving temp.: 48–53°

Caracole Saxo

Saxo is a lively beer, pale copper in color, with a persistent carbonation. A smack of spicy, almost peppery hops bursts from the glass. Some pale malt sweetness is evident on the palate, but the hops dominate the flavor, elegant but persistent, well into the drying finish.
Country: Belgium
ABV: 8%; Serving temp.: 48–53°

Huyghe Delirium Tremens

With pink elephants and dancing alligators on the label and a name that alludes to the perils of overindulgence, it's hard to take this beer seriously. Persevere though, noting the ripe banana and pear character and how it becomes bitter in the finish. A serious beer despite appearances.
Country: Belgium
ABV: 8.5%; Serving temp.: 48–53°

LIGHT / DARK
LIGHT-BODIED / FULL-BODIED

Brooklyn Local 1

Restlessly inventive brewmaster Garrett Oliver shows he can do Belgian too. In the strong golden ale style, this is full-bodied and slightly sweet, with some fruity notes (pear, banana) and a definite herbal edge. The finish is long and becomes dry and faintly spicy, with a lingering fruitiness.
Country: USA
ABV: 9%; Serving temp.: 48–53°

Urthel Hop-It

This beer is almost triple-like in its intensity. There's a spicy, medicinal edge, faint bubblegum, and a honeyed, estery aroma. The palate has a clean, pale malt fruitiness, with a layer of bitter hops all the way through and a long, bittersweet finish, with more honeyed notes in the aftertaste.

Food match: Thai-spiced chicken or pork, jerk chicken or fish
Country: Belgium
ABV: 9.5%; Serving temp.: 40–46

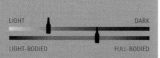

Hoegaarden Grand Cru

Being an all-malt brew, rather than mainly wheat, this can't be considered a premium version of Hoegaarden Wit, but it does share the same soft spiciness. A pale, slightly hazy beer, with bitter orange and coriander spice showing through in the long finish.
Country: Belgium
ABV: 8.5%; Serving temp.: 46–53°

Palm Royale

Midway between a triple and a blonde beer in style, strength, and intensity, this is a typically genre-defying Belgian beer—hard to classify, fun to drink. Sappy pale malt and an herbal hop quality to the aroma, sweetish on the tongue, with a peppery, bittersweet finish.
Country: Belgium
ABV: 7.5%; Serving temp.: 46–53°

De Dolle Brouwers Arabier

The bottled beers from De Dolle Brouwers can be very lively—this one soaked a rug as it burst forth with unusual force. The small amount of hazy gold beer that was left had a fruit and spice aroma (ripe cantaloupe, lemons, and black pepper) and a tangy bitter finish.
Country: Belgium
ABV: 7%; Serving temp.: 50–55°

Palm Brugge Triple

There is a nice aroma of apricots and spice to this hazy peachy-gold beer, along with a heady hint of alcohol. On the tongue is a burst of spritzy carbonation, and a fleeting sweetness quickly becomes dry, with the apricot fruitiness returning in the warming, bittersweet finish.
Country: Belgium
ABV: 8.7%; Serving temp.: 46–53°

Palm's Brugge beers were first brewed at De Gouden Boon, in the heart of Bruges' historic center

IPA

India Pale Ale (IPA) is a beer with a real history. The popular tale told about IPA is that it was a beer brewed in England for export to expatriates in India. It was (so the story goes) strong and hoppy so it would survive the rigors of the long sea voyage. The beer that emerged in India was in perfect condition and found much favor among appreciative drinkers there. Like all tales, there is some truth in there, but there is also a bit of myth too. It's true that some beers improved on the long journey to India, although to say that they were deliberately brewed strong and hoppy to withstand the journey is gilding the lily somewhat. Likewise, assertions that IPA has always been a strong style of beer are not completely correct, nor completely wrong. What can be said for certain (thanks to the online and published works of beer historians like Martyn Cornell and Ron Pattinson) is that IPAs tended to be more heavily hopped beers, with no particular bias to being strong.

However, no one ever let the facts get in the way of a good story. Regardless of history, IPA has come to be shorthand for a fairly strong beer with a good, bright hop character. Malt plays a supporting role, providing body and sweetness against which the hops are displayed to sometimes dazzling effect. While IPA may be English in origin, this is a style that the American craft brewing scene has taken and made its own. Some of the biggest, brightest, most striking IPAs are currently being brewed in the United States. These beers eschew the understated balance of classic ales and go all out for hop hit. To get more hops in, there has to be more malt against which to balance, and as a result, the alcohol levels rise precipitously. These are the Las Vegas of the beer world—bigger, brighter, more in-your-face, and likely to leave you waking up in the morning wondering what on earth happened last night.

Of course, as we've learned, good beer can be brewed anywhere. IPA has long since stopped being an English regional specialty and has become a way for brewers to cut loose and get wild with the hops. IPA is now brewed everywhere, and the notion of "authentic" IPA has been lost. Don't get me wrong—I'm no style slave, and this is one of my favorite styles of beer. However, IPA is now an international style of beer, and as such, the beers in this chapter should be thought of in those terms—IPA is rechristened here as International Pale Ale.

american pale ale

In some ways, I feel that making a distinction between American Pale Ale (APA) and other IPAs is a bit arbitrary. And yet when I look at this group of beers, I think that APA is a real category after all. The beers here all cluster very tightly in terms of flavor descriptors, and there is also an underplayed sense of restraint about them that makes other similar beers look like they are trying too hard. No one could accuse Sierra Nevada of not trying too hard—they pretty much created the style, set the benchmark, and then rolled it out to the world.

Hops growing in the Kootenai River Valley of Boundary County, Idaho

Sierra Nevada Pale Ale

With this beer, Sierra Nevada hit the holy grail, a craft beer with huge crossover potential. Copper-orange in color, with a zesty aroma of grapefruit and orange. The palate starts out toffeeish and slightly sweet, but the pithy hops add a layer of spicy dryness in the finish. A modern classic.

Food match: broiled or barbecued meat with a chile rub, or nachos with salsa
Country: USA
ABV: 5.6%; Serving temp.: 46-53°

Flying Dog Doggie Style Classic Pale Ale

Amber in color, and dry-hopped with (to quote the company website) "shit loads of Cascade hops," which are married to the intensity of the grapefruit, kumquat, and pine needle aromas and flavors present here. A nice nutty malt note shows through in the finish. Very drinkable.
Country: USA
ABV: 4.6%; Serving temp.: 46-53°

Firestone Walker Pale 31

Colored pale copper-gold, there is a pleasant balance to the nose of this beer, a mix of toffeeish malt and gently spicy hops. These flavors carry into the light-bodied palate, which carries a little orangey sweetness before a dry, spicy hop finish.
Country: USA
ABV: 4.8%; Serving temp.: 46-53°

Deschutes Mirror Pond Pale Ale

Copper-colored, with a zesty aroma—citrus and pine resin. On the palate is grapefruit, a little husky malt, and an airy quality that is hard to describe—it could almost be watermelon or cantaloupe. Finish is fairly dry. An enjoyably fresh take on the style.
Country: USA
ABV: 5%; Serving temp.: 46-53°

Shmaltz He'brew Genesis Ale

Copper-brown, with a nicely balanced, medium-toasted malt aroma. Good hop balance, with a nice firmness to the palate and an almost austere quality. Admirably unflashy, with a good toasted malt character. Very drinkable.
Country: USA
ABV: 5.6%; Serving temp.: 46-53°

IPA

IPA is an old style of beer, a beer with a lot of history attached to it, but somehow has come to define modern brewing. It seems as though everyone and their (Brew)dog has a bright, hoppy beer in their range, and for many it seems to be their flagship. What on earth did these people do before IPA? Brew less interesting beer, that's what. Beer-lovers everywhere should be taking advantage of the hop revolution that has happened—there has never been a greater variety of characterful, exciting-to-drink beers available to us. Here are some for your consideration.

A sack of dried hops ready for transportation to a brewery. Hoppy flavors are at the forefront of a good IPA.

🇳🇴 Haandbryggeriet IPA

I really like the Anglo-American international pale ale style, and this textbook example from Norway checks off all the right boxes for me. Big orange zest aroma? Check. Bittersweet orange marmalade on the palate? Check. Long, dry, orange pith finish? Check. Hard to find, but worth seeking out.

Food match: hot spice-rubbed broiled meat, with caramelized onions
Country: Norway
ABV: 6.5%; Serving temp.: 48–53°

✚ Thornbridge Jaipur

Even in a comically tiny font size, the list of awards this beer has won runs to a couple of pages. This golden IPA gives off huge tropical fruit aromas (pineapple, mango), which carry through into the sweetish palate. The finish starts sweet, but quickly evolves a dry, spicy bitterness.
Country: England
ABV: 5.9%; Serving temp.: 50–55°

✚ Outlaw Dead or Alive IPA

Outlaw, experimental arm of the celebrated Roosters Brewery, showcases the elegant power of American hops. A pale beer with fruity aromas—tangerine, kumquat, peach, and grapefruit. More of the same on the palate and the finish. Utterly delicious.
Country: England
ABV: 5%; Serving temp.: 50–55°

✚ St Austell Proper Job

The tide of British-inspired craft brewing in the US has washed back across the Atlantic. Proper Job is a great interpretation of the American IPA style—citrus and hopsack aromas fill the glass (lemon, grapefruit) and give a burst of lemon sherbet. Deliciously bitter finish.
Country: England
ABV: 5.5%; Serving temp.: 50–55°

🇺🇸 Speakeasy Untouchable Pale Ale

Pouring a hazy orange, this beer has a soft caramel and fruit aroma (orange, grapefruit, and apricot). On the tongue is sweet maltiness (hints of ripe apple and toffee), before a medium-dry finish. Orange-peel fruitiness persists, but doesn't dominate.
Country: USA
ABV: 6.5%; Serving temp.: 48–53°

🇦🇺 Little Creatures Pale Ale

Rather than go all out for a resinous hop hit, Little Creatures takes a more balanced approach. There is an almost tropical note to the nose (mango and pineapple), and the palate has a soft nutty malt quality that makes for a more rounded beer, vaguely reminiscent of a good English ale.

Food match: lightly spiced chicken with sweet potato, and a mango salsa
Country: Australia
ABV: 5.2%; Serving temp.: 46–53°

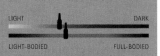

LIGHT   DARK
LIGHT-BODIED   FULL-BODIED

🇿🇦 Shongweni Robson's Durban Pale Ale

The aroma of this copper-gold beer has notes of pineapple, mango, and bitter orange, with a little toffee to boot. The beer is big and medium-sweet on the palate, with caramel, ripe fruit, and bitter orange leading the way to a long, full-bodied, and slightly nutty finish.
Country: South Africa
ABV: 5.7%; Serving temp.: 45–50°

LIGHT   DARK
LIGHT-BODIED   FULL-BODIED

🇦🇺 Asia Pacific Tui East India Pale Ale

It seems odd to describe this peachy-brown beer as an East India Pale ale given its low hop presence. However, it is quite complex—toffee and allspice, coffee notes mid-palate, with an autumnal overripe apple and pear quality. Perfectly nice.
Country: New Zealand
ABV: 4%; Serving temp.: 45–50°

LIGHT   DARK
LIGHT-BODIED   FULL-BODIED

🇲🇽 Cerveceria Mexicana Red Pig Mexican Ale

This copper-colored ale has a lovely aroma of caramel and roasted grain. The palate is medium-sweet, but a nice hop character keeps everything lively. The finish has more caramel, and citrus (even resinous) character.
Country: Mexico
ABV: 5%; Serving temp.: 45–50°

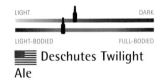

LIGHT   DARK
LIGHT-BODIED   FULL-BODIED

🇺🇸 Deschutes Twilight Ale

This is Deschutes' summer brew, created with a splendid lightness of touch. The pale malt and tropical fruit notes here are reminiscent of new pale golden English ales. Light-bodied and fruity, but refreshing, and crisp with passion fruit and guava.
Country: USA
ABV: 5%; Serving temp.: 45–50°

LIGHT   DARK
LIGHT-BODIED   FULL-BODIED

The Red Fort, former headquarters of the British Army in Delhi, which no doubt saw its fair share of IPA consumed by British colonists in India

Nørrebro Bryghus is a Copenhagen-based microbrewery whose café–restaurant brings fine beer to the city

Goose Island IPA

One of the first American IPAs I ever drank, and I still think it's a great example. Hazy orange in color, with a massive aroma of pine needles, marmalade, and dusty hopsack. On the tongue, caramel, burnt sugar, a dab of butterscotch, and a long resinous finish.

Food match: slow-cooked sticky pork ribs, strong Cheddar cheese, or barbecue
Country: USA
ABV: 5.9%; Serving temp.: 48-52°

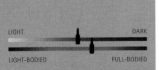

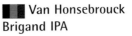 Van Honsebrouck Brigand IPA

As if it wasn't enough to have an English archer on its strong beer ("Brigand"), this brewery also produces very good (and weirdly authentic) British-style IPA. Resinous, peppery, orange-inflected hops dominate the aroma, and the palate is sweet, with a tangy bitter finish.
Country: Belgium
ABV: 6.5%; Serving temp.: 48-52°

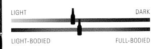

Burton Bridge Brewery Empire Pale Ale

Served blind, you might mistake this IPA for a Belgian strong ale—it has a surprising estery complexity on the nose. The palate, initially sweet, becomes dry in a series of fruity flavors (mango, apricot, apple), and builds into a medium-dry finish.
Country: England
ABV: 7.5%; Serving temp.: 50-55°

Nørrebro Bryghus Bombay Pale Ale

A trip to Copenhagen without visiting the Nørrebro Bryghus is a wasted opportunity. Excellent beer is brewed on-site, and the menus are Nordic-inflected classics. This copper-orange beer tips its hat in the direction of American IPAs, with a malty core and citrus-floral hop character.
Country: Denmark
ABV: 6.5%; Serving temp.: 48-52°

Meantime IPA

This copper-colored, champagne cork-stoppered beer seems to divide people, some finding the toffee malt, bitter orange, and dusty hopsack aromas offputting. Personally, I love the malty core overlaid by layer upon layer of resinous hops, becoming peppery and bittersweet in the finish.
Country: England
ABV: 7.5%; Serving temp.: 50-55°

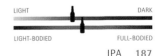

⚑ Highland Brewing Orkney Blast

Orange-gold, with a genuinely mouthwatering aroma of citrus zest (all of them, zingy as you like) and some background floral character. Bright, zesty attack, with lots of juicy fruit (apricot and orange). Big finish, spicy and slightly sweet. A great beer, perilously drinkable for the strength.

Food match: a perfect match for jerk chicken, with rice and peas
Country: Scotland
ABV: 6%; Serving temp.: 50–55°

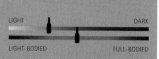

▀ Harpoon IPA

Pale gold in color, this looks almost like lager in the glass, but a quick sniff banishes this deception— there are pine needles and pineapples in abundance, with a little citrus pith thrown in for good measure. Fairly sweet on the palate, but finishes medium-dry with a long, zesty bitterness.
Country: USA
ABV: 5.9%; Serving temp.: 45–50°

⚑ Belhaven Twisted Thistle

Although Scotland is associated with sweeter, malty beers, aromas of orange, grapefruit, and dusty hopsack burst from this copper-gold IPA. The sweetly malty palate (grapefruit, tangerine) becomes more bitter and spicy in the finish.
Country: Scotland
ABV: 5.3%; Serving temp.: 50–55°

⚑ BrewDog Punk IPA

Take away all the brouhaha about controversial descriptions, authority-baiting names, and fancy labels, and what are you left with? Great beer, that's what. A fabulous golden IPA, with tropical fruit (pineapple, mango) on the nose, a sweetish palate, and a dry, grapefruity finish. An immodest classic.
Country: Scotland
ABV: 6%; Serving temp.: 50–55°

✚ Saltaire Cascade

Located on the edge of the UNESCO World Heritage site, Saltaire in West Yorkshire, the beers from this relatively new brewery are improving all the time. This pale golden ale has a lovely, sweet, floral quality and a gentle pine-needle finish. English ale with an American accent.
Country: England
ABV: 4.8%; Serving temp.: 50–55°

The Harpoon Brewery, on the Boston waterfront, is New England's largest craft brewery

A head of yeast in a large fermenter

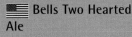 Bells Two Hearted Ale

Copper-gold, with a massive aroma of earthy, wet, resinous hops. The palate is medium-sweet, displaying a fruity malt presence overlaid with a big hop character that comes across like orange and ginger marmalade. Spicy, exciting, and distinctive, with a zesty lemongrass note to the finish. Excellent.

Food match: dry, spicy foods—tandoori chicken, Buffalo wings, even well-spiced tacos
Country: USA
ABV: 7%; Serving temp.: 46–50°

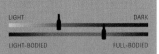

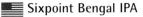 Sixpoint Bengal IPA

There is a crunchy hop aroma to this copper-gold IPA, but unlike a lot of "me too" IPAs, there is also a good malt presence. The citrus zest and toffee character carries through to the palate where, although the hops become prominent, the malt still plays a supporting role.
Country: USA
ABV: 6.8%; Serving temp.: 45–50°

Mt. Shasta Mountain High IPA

Hazy copper-orange, with a faint alcohol note alongside an appetizing tangerine and pine needle aroma. Medium-bodied, with a soft sweetness mid-palate. This sweetness carries into the finish, where it merges with hop bitterness. Tasty.
Country: USA
ABV: 7%; Serving temp.: 46–53°

Stone IPA

This copper-colored IPA has a mouthwatering marmalade and sherbet aroma. There is an explosion of orange sherbet mid-palate, kept in check by a big pithy bitterness. The beer turns dry, spicy, and resinous in the finish, with a persistent bitter-orange note. Perhaps one of the best of the style.
Country: USA
ABV: 6.9%; Serving temp.: 45–50°

Dogfish Head 60 Minute IPA

"60 minute" refers to the length of time the wort is boiled, when hops are added every five minutes via a device christened "Sir Hops-A-Lot." The hazy copper-colored beer is a riot of citrus, pine, and bittersweet fruitiness. A real must-try beer.
Country: USA
ABV: 6%; Serving temp.: 45–50°

🇺🇸 Victory Hop Devil

Copper-red in color, this IPA has a lovely robust malt note to its aroma. The tropical fruit notes in the aroma show up in the palate (mango, papaya), with some bitter orange and an ever-present malty backbone. The finish has an enjoyably fruity malt quality.

Food match: steak and caramelized onions, or broiled steak burrito
Country: USA
ABV: 6.7%; Serving temp.: 45–50°

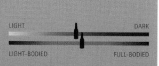

🇺🇸 Speakeasy Big Daddy IPA

Hazy copper-gold, with a huge, vibrant aroma that leaps from the glass—orange (zest and fruit), pine needles, dusty hopsack, and a hint of toasted grain in the background. On the palate is a burst of resinous bittersweetness, fading to a tangy bitterness.
Country: USA
ABV: 6.5%; Serving temp.: 45–50°

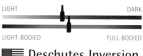

🇺🇸 Deschutes Inversion IPA

There is a note of orange pith to the dry, medium-bodied, and fairly bitter palate, which is also in the aroma alongside hints of alcohol. The color suggests darker roast malts, confirmed by the toffee caramel notes. Persistent and bitter finish.
Country: USA
ABV: 6.8%; Serving temp.: 45–50°

🇺🇸 Flying Dog Snake Dog IPA

The intensity is turned up a notch here, with nutty crystal malt evident in the aroma, along with the sort of hop character that suggests the hopsacks have been slashed open with a jagged blade and, with hoppy entrails bursting forth, tossed whole into the conditioning tank.
Country: USA
ABV: 5.6%; Serving temp.: 46–53°

🇩🇰 Mikkeller All Others Pale

A hazy copper-gold color, with a mouthwatering aroma of zesty, resinous hops, along with a touch of dusty hopsack. A fresh, resinous hop attack sweeps in mid-palate, taking the flavor from medium-sweet to spicy, dry, and bitter. Very enjoyable.
Country: Denmark
ABV: 6%; Serving temp.: 46–53°

Prohibition-themed "speakeasy" bars (and beer brands) have flourished in recent years

double/imperial IPA

The term "double" or "imperial" can be attached to any beer style. Purists say it doesn't really mean anything (they're right), but still, it has come to signify a beer that is brewed with an unusually large amount of malt and hops. This, as I'm sure you will have worked out, means that it is very full-flavored and usually high in alcohol. The examples here are all unusually intense and will make anything else you drink afterward taste of nothing—unless it's a triple / intergalactic IPA (it will happen eventually).

Rye, still a staple crop in eastern Europe, is sometimes used by brewers for color and flavor. It can add a spicy, herbal edge to the beer.

🇺🇸 Shmaltz He'brew Bittersweet Lenny's RIPA

The very intense nose on this dark copper-brown beer has a hint of aniseed (from the rye?) sitting atop a huge nutty toffee aroma, with citrus zest too. The sweet palate moves slowly into huge bitterness via toffee, golden raisins, orange, and winter spice. Intense, enormous, and a lot of fun.

Food match: hearty rib-sticking food—baked enchiladas or lasagna
Country: USA
ABV: 10%; Serving temp.: 45–50*

LIGHT — DARK
LIGHT-BODIED — FULL-BODIED

🇺🇸 Port Brewing Hop 15

Huge hoppy aromas (pine needles, orange, black pepper) leap from the glass. There is a marmalade sweetness before the hops continue their fiendish fandango on the tongue. Finish is long, bittersweet, with a warming alcoholic glow. Alarmingly enjoyable.
Country: USA
ABV: 10.5%; Serving temp.: 45–50°

LIGHT — DARK

LIGHT-BODIED — FULL-BODIED

🇺🇸 Victory Hop Wallop

Victory's annual hymn of praise to the hop harvest, and my, they sing loud in Downington. A pale golden ale with a penetrating fruity aroma—tropical fruit, grapefruit zest, and a little kumquat hold an impromptu hoedown on your tongue, in the nicest possible way.
Country: USA
ABV: 8.5%; Serving temp.: 43–50°

LIGHT — DARK

LIGHT-BODIED — FULL-BODIED

🇺🇸 Speakeasy Double Daddy Imperial IPA

The intense aroma to this amber-gold IPA is reminiscent of rubbed fresh hops—seriously resinous and almost chokingly pungent. The palate is medium-sweet, with tropical fruit (mango, pineapple, melon), lemon sherbet, and pine. Finishes big and bittersweet.
Country: USA
ABV: 9.5%; Serving temp.: 45–50°

LIGHT — DARK
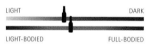
LIGHT-BODIED — FULL-BODIED

🇺🇸 Great Divide Titan IPA

This copper-gold IPA is almost disastrously drinkable. So enjoyable are the grapefruit aromas, and pine needle hops with bittersweet finish that I drank four in very quick succession once. This resulted in a peaceful, but sunburnt slumber.
Country: USA
ABV: 6.8%; Serving temp.: 45–50°

LIGHT — DARK

LIGHT-BODIED — FULL-BODIED

trappist & abbey beers

There's no denying that there is something special about the notion of beer brewed by monks. The thought of these men, leading cloistered lives of work and prayer in the service of their god, pausing occasionally to fire up the brew kettle to create something really special—well, it has a bit more romance to it than an anonymous industrial unit on the outskirts of a city, doesn't it?

The "Trappist" denomination for beer is a protected mark that can be used by only seven Trappist breweries, all located at monasteries. There are six in Belgium (Chimay, Westmalle, Orval, Rochefort, Achel, and Westvleteren) and one just across the border in Holland (La Trappe). In one way, it is odd to try to talk about Trappist beers as a homogenous group, as each brewery has a slightly idiosyncratic output. The quality overall is high, but stylistically, they don't really hang together as a group of beers. Conversely, the aura that surrounds them (perhaps like a halo surrounding a saint) is such that they are revered by beer drinkers everywhere.

This aura and influence has led to a group of beers that pay homage to these classics. Abbey beers are a category that can fairly easily be classified according to strength and color—single, double (or dubbel), triple (or tripel), and quadrupel. These categories are thought to hark back to the days of low literacy, when beers were marked with a number of Xs to indicate strength, with four Xs being the strongest (although it's probably only a matter of time before an exuberant American craft brewer creates the quintuple style). Singles are ordinary blonde beers, around 6%abv. Doubles are dark beers (like a brune), around the same strength. Triples are pale, around 8%abv, while quadrupels tend to be tawny (rather than dark) and around 10%abv. Although many abbey beers fall neatly into these style descriptors, the Trappist beers don't. Westmalle makes a dubbel and a tripel, and only La Trappe produces the full range from single (their blonde beer) through to a quadrupel.

A few abbey beers are manufactured and distributed on a large scale, although that doesn't necessarily mean that they are not interesting beers—on the contrary, they are an excellent starting point on the road to beer appreciation. The Trappist beers can be harder to find, although La Trappe and Chimay are fairly widely distributed these days. The pinnacle of beer hunterdom are the beers of Westvleteren, which are hard to find and rated by many as being among the best beers in the world. Although they are not meant to be resold once purchased from the abbey, I'm sure that even the brothers of the abbey at Westvleteren might feel a touch of the sin of pride at how the fruits of their labor are received in the secular world.

abbey blonde beer

As you might expect from a category of beers that includes any Belgian beers, even though the beers featured here are all classed as blonde beers, there is a big variety of flavors. However, they are very accessible, easy to understand, and have a full-bodied, but unchallenging, character. Leffe Blonde is the most widely found example; however, some look down on it, being the product of a huge multinational brewing corporation. Truth be told, there is nothing wrong with it, and it's a good introduction to the style. A couple more examples can be found in the next spread.

The cafés on the Grand' Place in Brussels are the perfect place to enjoy a Belgian abbey beer

Ename Blonde

Blonde beer tends to get a bad press as merely a simple introduction to Belgian beer, but this beer changes that. The yeasty spiciness has an herbal edge, and the palate has a good hoppy complexity. Being unpasteurized and unfiltered means a lot of character is left in. Very good.

Food match: grilled fish or chicken, or a bowl of nuts in a bar in Brussels
Country: Belgium
ABV: 6.5%; Serving temp.: 45–50°

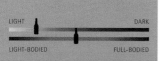

Grimbergen Blonde

Soft and rounded, this pin-bright golden beer is a favorite standby of mine when vacationing in France. For some reason, it's everywhere. Medium-sweet on the tongue, with a nourishing, malty quality. It has a little more dryness to the finish than many of the other blonde beers.
Country: Belgium
ABV: 6.7%; Serving temp.: 41–44°

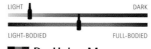

De Halve Maan Brugse Zot

The rich, slightly yeasty spiciness and full fruity esters (bananas) to the nose of this golden blonde beer set it slightly above many other similar examples. The palate is medium-sweet, with some toffee spicy hop dryness in the finish.
Country: Belgium
ABV: 6%; Serving temp.: 45–50°

Leffe Blonde

The sweet, full-bodied maltiness of the polished golden Leffe Blonde is a nice example of the style, despite enormous production figures. The spiced pale malt aroma (coriander) leads to a sweetish, fruity palate (banana, ripe apple) and a long finish with very little bitterness.
Country: Belgium
ABV: 6.6%; Serving temp.: 41–44°

Moortgat Maredsous 6

Alongside a lemony note, there's a sappy malt aroma to this medium-gold blonde beer that has a lot in common with Moortgat's flagship beer, Duvel. On the palate, it has a restrained hop presence, with some nice spicy character and sweet finish.
Country: Belgium
ABV: 6%; Serving temp.: 45–50°

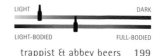

abbey & trappist tripel

Tripels are fabulously enjoyable beers. There is something very grown-up about them; from the higher alcohol to the slightly herbal bitterness that many of them display, they are certainly not to be trifled with. They are good to drink on their own, although the strength makes this something of an ill-fated activity. One of my favorite food and beer pairings is broiled asparagus with a well-chilled Westmalle Tripel—the bitterness of the Westmalle accentuates the charred notes and the pungent herbal character of the asparagus. As I said, a grown-up pleasure, but one worth taking time to enjoy.

Entrance of the Sint Sixtus abbey in Westvleteren, brewers of the world's best Trappist beer

Bosteels Tripel Karmeliet

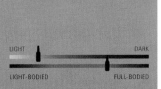

This pale, slightly hazy, multigrain (malt, wheat, and oats) beer has a really appealing aroma of peaches and apricots. The oats give the beer a fuller mouthfeel, and the medium-sweet palate gives way to a fairly long, drying finish. A much underrated classic.

Food match: strong soft cheese, mussels, pâtés, and terrines
Country: Belgium
ABV: 8.4%; **Serving temp.:** 45–50°

LIGHT   DARK
LIGHT-BODIED   FULL-BODIED

La Trappe Blond

A bright golden beer with a full, malty aroma (honey, caramel) and some doughy notes. Medium-sweet on the tongue, with a well-judged level of complexity—not too demanding, but enough yeasty spiciness and pear and faintly floral notes to keep things interesting. Finishes fruity, rounded, and medium-dry.
Country: Holland
ABV: 6.5%; **Serving temp.:** 46–53°

LIGHT   DARK
LIGHT-BODIED   FULL-BODIED

Van Steenberge Augustijn

In the tripel style, this copper-gold beer has a slightly medicinal edge alongside the hop aroma, and a spirity quality too. Dry and lively on the tongue, with some pale malt character and a faint note of scorched sugar alongside the punchy, bitter hop finish.
Country: Belgium
ABV: 7%; **Serving temp.:** 44–50°

LIGHT   DARK
LIGHT-BODIED   FULL-BODIED

't IJ Zatte

The slightly acetic aroma is characteristic of wild yeast, but odd to find in a tripel. The dryish palate has got a lot going on—bitter orange, coriander, and a slightly funky, tart quality. The finish is dry and complex, with good persistence, showing spice and more bitter orange.
Country: Holland
ABV: 8%; **Serving temp.:** 42–46°

LIGHT   DARK
LIGHT-BODIED   FULL-BODIED

Du Bocq Corsendonk Agnus-Tripel

Pours a pale straw color, with a really appealing aroma—pale malt, yeast, and spiced bread. In the mouth, Agnus has a smooth malty palate, with a suggestion of elderflower and a sweetish, medium-length finish. No frills, just a quality, blonde abbey beer.
Country: Belgium
ABV: 7.5%; **Serving temp.:** 44–50°

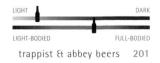

LIGHT   DARK
LIGHT-BODIED   FULL-BODIED

 Unibroue La Fin Du Monde

A full-bodied interpretation of the tripel style from this Belgian-founded Canadian brewery. The aroma hints at classic Belgian spices (coriander, Curaçao, although the beer isn't actually spiced), while the palate is full and fairly sweet, with some drying bitterness in the finish.

Food match: seafood soup with rouille, cold poached chicken with curried mayonnaise
Country: Canada
ABV: 9%; Serving temp.: 45–50°

LIGHT | DARK

LIGHT-BODIED | FULL-BODIED

Leffe Triple

Some enthusiasts dismiss Leffe out of hand, on the assumption that big breweries only make bad beer. Forget what they say; this is a perfectly good example of the style. Spicy and slightly medicinal on the nose, with a soft fruitiness to the palate, and finishing initially sweet, then becoming bitter.
Country: Belgium
ABV: 8.5%; Serving temp.: 46–50°

LIGHT | DARK

LIGHT-BODIED | FULL-BODIED

Victory Golden Monkey

An almost comically Belgian aroma leaps from the glass—pear, grape, some citrus, and an herbal, medicinal hop quality. Candy sugar is evident throughout, alongside a huge, mouth-filling flavor. Pale malt fruitiness and a medium-sweet palate dry to a pleasantly bitter finish.
Country: USA
ABV: 9.5%; Serving temp.: 45–50°

LIGHT | DARK

LIGHT-BODIED | FULL-BODIED

 Westvleteren Blond

Soft pale malt aroma, with some lemony hops and a faint note of wild yeast fermentation (brettanomyces?). Complex palate of medium-sweet pale malt and tart lemon pith, with some hop bitterness building in the finish. Simultaneously complex and easy to drink, pitched somewhere between a blonde and a tripel. Excellent.
Country: Belgium
ABV: 5.8%; Serving temp.: 50–56°

LIGHT | DARK

LIGHT-BODIED | FULL-BODIED

La Trappe Tripel

Pale malt, spice, and a faint suggestion of toffee (clearly some sugar is used in the brew kettle) lead to a sweetish palate. If the start all seems a bit obvious, that changes on the swallow; a soft bitterness and notes of crystallized angelica emerge in the finish.
Country: Holland
ABV: 8%; Serving temp.: 45–50°

LIGHT | DARK

LIGHT-BODIED | FULL-BODIED

Historic Leuven, Belgium. Much of the town is now dominated by the Stella Artois Brewery, where Leffe is also brewed.

Simple but sophisticated foods, such as grilled asparagus, make a great match with fine Trappist beers

Val-Dieu Triple

This is a great example of a classic style. Pale malt fruitiness (peaches, pears) and a slightly medicinal lemony hop note are evident on the nose. The palate has just the right amount of sweetness, before a fruity (more peaches and pears), slightly peppery, and gently bitter finish.

Food match: white meat in cream sauce, endive with pear and Roquefort salad
Country: Belgium
ABV: 9%; Serving temp.: 45-50°

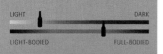

Urthel Hibernus Quentum Tripel

There's a lovely balanced, rounded quality to this tripel that is sometimes lacking in lesser examples. The spirity aroma carries a good amount of fruit (pear, orange) and a honeyed, floral edge. The palate is intense, with peach, honey, and peppery hops that carry into the finish.
Country: Belgium
ABV: 9%; Serving temp.: 45-50°

Alvinne Tripel

This hazy copper-gold beer packs quite a punch, and not just via the alcohol. The aroma is brightly fruity (bitter orange, apricot), and these flavors carry into the lively palate. Medium-sweet, with a bitter orange marmalade note to finish. An unusual tripel, but very enjoyable.
Country: Belgium
ABV: 8.7%; Serving temp.: 48-52°

Van Den Bossche Lamoral Tripel

It's unlikely that beers this strong can display delicacy, but there is an airy floral quality to this beer that makes it very drinkable. Sure, there is a touch of alcohol warmth, some nice hops too, and the honeyed, orange blossom character makes it noteworthy.
Country: Belgium
ABV: 8%; Serving temp.: 45-50°

Moortgat Maredsous 10

There is an herbal, almost medicinal intensity to this copper-gold beer that puts many more expensive examples of the style to shame. The palate has a candy-sugar edge with plenty of spicy hops. The finish is long, turning dry, with alcohol warmth.
Country: Belgium
ABV: 10%; Serving temp.: 45-50°

◼◼ Westmalle Tripel

Westmalle Tripel is pale straw-gold in color and has an intense, herbal hop nose, with a hint of savory spices (perhaps coriander and black pepper). It is lively in the mouth, with a pleasing dry bitterness and a medium-intense, slightly herbal/savory finish. Viewed by many as the classic of the style.

Food match: broiled asparagus with shaved Parmesan and ground black pepper
Country: Belgium
ABV: 9.5%; Serving temp.: 46-54°

LIGHT ▮ DARK
LIGHT-BODIED ▮ FULL-BODIED

◼◼ Achelse Kluis Achel Blonde

The beers from Achel seem to be getting better as years go by. I recall this tripel as being markedly sweeter a few years ago. Although there is still a little peachy sweetness mid-palate, the long, drying finish now has a very grown-up herbal bitterness to it.
Country: Belgium
ABV: 8%; Serving temp.: 45-50°

LIGHT ▮ DARK
LIGHT-BODIED ▮ FULL-BODIED

◼◼ Het Anker Gouden Carolus Tripel

There is a worrying drinkability to this strong golden beer. Lovely soft texture, some spice (coriander), apricot and peach notes, some sweetness mid-palate, and then a bittersweet sunshine quality. A personal favorite.
Country: Belgium
ABV: 9%; Serving temp.: 45-50°

LIGHT ▮ DARK
LIGHT-BODIED ▮ FULL-BODIED

◼◼ Chimay White

Chimay White (in larger corked bottles, Cinq Cents or "Five Hundred," referring to the town's fifth centennial) is one of the few Trappist beers that exhibits a pronounced hop character. The bready aroma and slightly wild, herbal note in the nose point the way to a spicy, bittersweet palate and pronounced dry finish.
Country: Belgium
ABV: 8%; Serving temp.: 47-52°

LIGHT ▮ DARK
LIGHT-BODIED ▮ FULL-BODIED

◼◼ De Struise & Mikkeller Elliot Brew

Billed as a "RateBeer Special Release" and produced for the "international community of beer tasters." The tangy orange hops, intense citrus-pith fruitiness, spicy finish (nutmeg), and alcohol glow are sure to win plaudits.
Country: Belgium
ABV: 9%; Serving temp.: 47-52°

LIGHT ▮ DARK
LIGHT-BODIED ▮ FULL-BODIED

Castle in the Belgian village of Westmalle, home to one of the most famous Trappist breweries

abbey & trappist dubbel

There is a full, chunky, solid quality to a good dubbel that you
don't get from any other style of beer. The darker malts and
moderate strength ensure a medium-sweet and fairly fruity beer.
While there are the Trappist classics to explore, don't fall into the
trap of thinking that these are the only dubbels worth drinking. For
example, the abbey beers of St. Bernardus are outstanding quality,
and the brunes featured here (you could almost use brune and dubbel
interchangeably) are all very acceptable, not least the very enjoyable
Pelforth Brune, a French holiday beer par excellence.

Roasting barley adds a dark color and roasted flavor to a beer, but does not affect alcohol content

◼◼ St. Bernardus Tripel

The floral, spiced note to the nose of this amber-gold beer is a bit deceptive, as you could almost mistake it for a good-quality blonde beer. On the palate, things tighten up a little, with peach and orange notes before a medium-dry finish. Light, fruity and worryingly easy to drink.

Food match: broiled goat cheese with lemon-dressed mesclun salad
Country: Belgium
ABV: 8%; Serving temp.: 45–50°

◼◼ Van Steenberge Augustijn Grand Cru

This very pale golden ale has a lot of floral and fruity aromatics to it—jasmine and apricots are easily discernible. The palate is initially medium-sweet, but a soft bitterness builds into the finish, where a little sweetness remains alongside a floral note and a zesty lemon twist.
Country: Belgium
ABV: 9%; Serving temp.: 45–50°

◼◼ Du Bocq Corsendonk Pater-Dubbel

Dark brown with ruby highlights, Pater has a malt character with a burst of sweetish coffee and caramel mid-palate, leading to a surprisingly dry finish with burnt, smoky, and bitter edges. Simple, but still enjoyable.
Country: Belgium
ABV: 7.5%; Serving temp.: 45–50°

◼◼ De Halve Maan Bruges Zot Dubbel

There's a heady, perfumed quality to this lovely ruddy-brown ale that's hard to identify—a combination of malt loaf, winter spice, and beeswax candle. That doesn't make it sound very appealing, does it? Full-flavored, malty, and complex, finishing surprisingly dry. Very good.
Country: Belgium
ABV: 7.5%; Serving temp.: 45–50°

◼◼ Ename Dubbel

It's hard to believe that a ruddy-brown beer can have such a lightness of touch, but that is the case here. There is a little malt fruitiness to the nose, some dried fruit to the palate, and a faint woody smokiness to the finish, but the overall impression here is of delicacy and balance.
Country: Belgium
ABV: 6.5%; Serving temp.: 45–50°

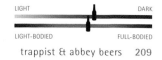

trappist & abbey beers   209

Leffe Radieuse

The name means "halo," and I suppose the glow you get after a couple of these might just be mistaken for a divine aura. There is a slightly heady quality to this coppery-brown beer, a suggestion of liqueur-soaked cherries and rumtopf, and a fruity bittersweet finish.

Food match: terrine (preferably game) with sweet chutney and black bread
Country: Belgium
ABV: 8.2%; Serving temp.: 40–45°

Leffe Brune

Despite the brooding mahogany color of this big-production beer, there isn't a great deal to distinguish it from its blonde sibling. The familiar spiced aroma has a slight hint of dark fruit and smoke, while the sweetish palate ends with the suggestion of roasted grain bitterness.
Country: Belgium
ABV: 6.5%; Serving temp.: 40–45°

't IJ Natte

There is a surprising lightness of touch to this beer, given that stylistically this is a dubbel. The characteristic 't IJ wildness is present on the nose, but it works in harmony with some light spice notes (coriander). The fruity palate finishes slightly tart, with spice and bitter orange notes.
Country: Holland
ABV: 6.5%; Serving temp.: 45–50°

Moortgat Maredsous 8

Alongside the dried fruit and coffee aromas in this mahogany-colored beer, there is a hint of something savory (soy sauce? barbecue sauce?). The palate is drier than expected, with a tart edge and a suggestion of wild yeast. Medium-dry, nutty finish.
Country: Belgium
ABV: 8%; Serving temp.: 45–50°

Pelforth Brune

Brune came as a real eye-opener when I was on vacation in France a few years ago. A rich red-brown color, it has a pleasing, dark, fruity, malt aroma, with a little earthy spiciness. The palate is quite sweet, although not overly so, and the candy-sugar finish is dry and smoky.
Country: France
ABV: 6.5%; Serving temp.: 45–50°

Rich, sweet meaty dishes such as venison are a good partner to dark abbey ales

Many Belgian abbeys and monasteries fell into disrepair in the 1790s; others were bolstered by French emigrants who brought brewing expertise with them

St. Bernardus Pater 6

There is a wonderfully doughy note to the aroma of this pale brown beer that brings to mind a bakery that is about to start baking. Yeast and honey on the nose, with a soft hint of toffee to the palate. Some dryness in the finish, surprisingly light-bodied and delicate.

Food match: oxtail stew, duck with black cherry or hoisin sauce
Country: Belgium
ABV: 6.7%; Serving temp.: 45-50°

LIGHT — DARK

LIGHT-BODIED — FULL-BODIED

Westmalle Dubbel

Westmalle Dubbel is ruddy brown with ruby highlights. The darker malts and brown sugars used give this medium-bodied beer flavors of dried fruit and a hint of cocoa in the finish. Recent bottlings seem to be drier than I remember, but the beer still has a sweetish edge.
Country: Belgium
ABV: 7%; Serving temp.: 45-50°

Achelse Kluis Achel Brune

This mahogany beer strikes a lovely balance between monastic reserve and accessibility. The dark malt nose has a hint of cherries and grapes. The palate is initially sweet, with some dried fruit, but dries fairly quickly, leaving roasted malt bitterness.
Country: Belgium
ABV: 8%; Serving temp.: 45-50°

La Trappe Dubbel

Now firmly back in the Trappist fold after a brief period of corporate exile, La Trappe is the most accessible range of Trappist ales. Dubbel has aromas of burnt caramel and spice (coriander), a sweet palate with a slightly smoky note, and a drier finish than the palate suggests.
Country: Holland
ABV: 7%; Serving temp.: 45-50°

St. Bernardus Prior 8

Medium-dark brown in color, with a lovely malty aroma of fruit, bread, and caramel. The rich smoothness of the palate is a real treat, showing more dried fruit, a little honey, and some nutty notes in the slightly warming and surprisingly dry finish.
Country: Belgium
ABV: 8%; Serving temp.: 45-50°

trappist & abbey beers   213

trappist ale

This spread is all about one beer—Orval. It's odd that such a seemingly singular beer—dry, peppery, and becoming fusty with brettanomyces funk over time—should inspire such fervent homage. But then again, it really is a beer for connoisseurs; you need to know a bit about the beer to enjoy it fully. Mikkeller and Goose Island are laying their cards on the table with their interpretations, demonstrating that they understand what makes Orval great, with their own particular twist. Incredibly, the version that Mikkeller has managed to produce almost eclipses the original's greatness. Almost....

The abbey at Orval, where written records prove beer has been brewed since at least the 1600s

■■ Orval Orval

The Abbey Notre-Dame d'Orval is unique in the Trappist pantheon in that it produces only one beer, but what a beer! It is triple-fermented, hazy, and copper-colored, with a distinct dry hop character. The presence of brettanomyces yeast means that aged examples develop a dry complexity, with a characteristic "horse blanket" aroma. A true original.

Food match: a great apéritif, or serve with cold cuts or wild mushroom pasta
Country: Belgium
ABV: 6.2%; **Serving temp.:** 52–57°

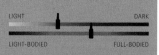

▇▇ Goose Island Matilda

Another tribute (along with Mikkeller's It's Alive!) to the Trappist classic, Orval. Copper-colored, with a soft, sappy aroma (ripe fruit, spice, pine needles). Some complex spiciness mid-palate, before a long, medium-sweet finish that has some characterful bitterness.
Country: USA
ABV: 7%; **Serving temp.:** 50–55°

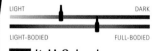

▬▬ 't IJ Columbus

The slightly wild edge to this brewery's beers can be challenging, but it makes sense here. The tart acetic nose sits well with the aroma of peach and strawberry. On the palate, there are layers of fruit (more peach), floral notes, and sour lemon. Very complex and very enjoyable.
Country: Holland
ABV: 9%; **Serving temp.:** 50–55°

■■ Mikkeller It's Alive!

Another of Mikkeller's homages that almost eclipses the object of its affections (in this case, Orval). Hazily copper-colored, with a big zesty (orange, grapefruit) aroma, and a touch of brettanomyces funkiness. Medium-dry, with a big burst of hops and more brett on the palate. Long finish, with bitterness building.
Country: Denmark
ABV: 8%; **Serving temp.:** 50–55°

■■ Chimay Red

Perhaps the most widely available of the Trappist beers, Chimay Red has an inviting aroma of red and dark berries. In the mouth, brewing sugar is immediately apparent as a sweet fruitiness, with some hop dryness arriving late in the day to perk things up a bit.
Country: Belgium
ABV: 7%; **Serving temp.:** 53–57°

dark trappist ale

This is where it all starts to get a bit serious. Although it's nice to have nomenclature like dubbel and tripel,  sometimes there isn't really a style to pigeonhole a group of beers, but just a description of their physical attributes. The Trappist beers from Rochefort don't really divide by style, only by strength, gaining intensity as you move up the scale; the 10 is regarded as a classic, although I prefer the rounded drinkability of the 8. We'll talk more about the revered, almost mythical beers of Westvleteren in the next spread.

Dark beer and strong cheese—a classic combination

Rochefort
Rochefort 8

Rochefort 8 is a tawny brown color, with a complex nose of brown bread and bananas. On the tongue, a riot of fruitiness and malt notes—dates, toasted bread, coffee, and sherry. The finish is long and fairly drying, with just a little noticeable alcohol. Easy to drink for such a big beer.

Food match: pâtés, strong cheeses, hearty stews
Country: Belgium
ABV: 9.2%; Serving temp.: 50-55°

LIGHT | DARK
LIGHT-BODIED | FULL-BODIED

Chimay Blue

Chimay Blue (Grande Reserve in larger corked bottles) is a dark copper beer with caramel and winter spice on the nose, an assertive malt loaf character mid-palate, and a gentle bump of warming alcohol in the slowly drying finish. Some critics claim Chimay beers have deteriorated, but they are still very enjoyable.
Country: Belgium
ABV: 9%; Serving temp.: 50-55°

LIGHT | DARK
LIGHT-BODIED | FULL-BODIED

Westvleteren Extra 8

This august ale is great young, but it becomes stunning with age. Russet in color, it has an aroma of plums, liqueur-soaked cherries, and cognac in its youth. With age, it gains an amazing complexity of honey, nuts, beeswax, and medicinal edge.
Country: Belgium
ABV: 8%; Serving temp.: 50-55°

LIGHT | DARK
LIGHT-BODIED | FULL-BODIED

Rochefort
Rochefort 10

Looking almost like cola as it is poured, Rochefort 10 is dark with ruddy highlights. The nose hints at figs, sour plums, and dark chocolate. The beer is big but balanced in the mouth, with dark fruit, coffee, dark chocolate, and a suggestion of whiskey in the finish. A world-class beer.
Country: Belgium
ABV: 11.3%; Serving temp.: 50-55°

LIGHT | DARK
LIGHT-BODIED | FULL-BODIED

Rochefort
Rochefort 6

Copper-brown in color, Rochefort 6's aromas of caramel and dried fruit (apricots and golden raisins) leap from the glass on pouring. Lighter-bodied than one might expect, this beer has a balanced, bittersweet character reminiscent of strong English ale.
Country: Belgium
ABV: 7.5%; Serving temp.: 50-55°

LIGHT | DARK
LIGHT-BODIED | FULL-BODIED

trappist & abbey beers 217

trappist & abbey quadrupel

The journey up the intensity scale from dubbel to tripel must logically conclude with quadrupel. Included here is a Westvleteren 12, revered by many as the best beer in the world. It could be that its rarity value contributes to this exalted status—it is sold only from the abbey, on the condition that it not be resold for profit. Of course, it changes hands many times after this transaction, and I'm almost (but not quite) ashamed to say that I too have indulged in this illicit trade, conscientiously ensuring that bottles are not resold by drinking any that I happen to find.

Deeply savory yet fruity foods—such as duck breast in cherry sauce—combine well with trappist beers

Westvleteren Abt 12

This beer is regarded by many as the best in the world, due partly to its rarity, but also because it's delicious and ages spectacularly well. Figs, raisins, and plums jostle each other in the aroma, while the palate is sweetly figgy, drying through nutty toffee to an almost savory crescendo.

Food match: duck breast with cherry or orange sauce, or as a digestif
Country: Belgium
ABV: 10.2%; Serving temp.: 50–55°

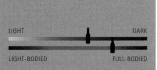

St. Bernardus Abt 12

The heady aroma to this reddish brown beer has dried fruit, caramel, and a rich, sweetly perfumed edge. The palate is soft, rounded, and smooth, with a heady, floral quality, alongside some ripe plums, toffee, and licorice. Some warmth is evident in the medium-dry finish.
Country: Belgium
ABV: 10%; Serving temp.: 50–55°

Grimbergen Optimo Bruno

If you were being inattentive, and mistook the word "Bruno" for brune, you'd be impressed at how much flavor was in this beer—spirit-soaked cherries, sweet stewed fruit, and chocolate with some bitter hops in the finish. Beware: delicious but deadly.
Country: Belgium
ABV: 10%; Serving temp.: 50–55°

La Trappe Quadrupel

Sweet dried fruits and cough drops prevail in the aroma of this coppery beer. The palate exhibits a telltale hit of warm alcohol, along with a faintly medicinal licorice quality and more pale dried fruit. The finish is bittersweet, with overripe fruit.
Country: Holland
ABV: 10%; Serving temp.: 50–55°

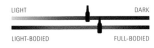

Urthel Samaranth Quadrupel

There is debate as to whether quadrupel is a "real" style or not, but it's a handy way of knowing what you're in for. Tawny-colored, with lots of toffee and dried fruit character; a big, fruity palate with some cognac notes; and a big, warming finish.
Country: Belgium
ABV: 11.5%; Serving temp.: 50–55°

barley wine & old ale

Old ale and barley wine are rolled together in this chapter; even though the outliers in each category are substantially different from each other, there is also a lot of crossover between the two. At the crossover point, where it is hard to tell whether a beer is a barley wine or old ale, you might expect to find a beer that is around 8%abv, mid to dark brown, with a fairly sweet, malty palate. At the extremes of each category, you can find an old ale that is almost stout-black, weighing in at 4.6%abv, and a copper-gold barley wine tipping the scales at 11.5%abv.

To clearly define old ale is difficult, but a typical example might be around 5%abv, ruddy dark brown, with a fruity malt character and a little dryness. There should definitely be something warming and restorative about it—not necessarily an alcohol warmth, but a hearty, chewy quality that makes more sense when it is drunk in front of an open fire, in an English country pub, on a cold winter's evening. There is something about it (not just the alcohol) that helps to drive out the cold.

There is also a traditional variant of old ale that is matured in wood, and as a consequence develops a certain complexity from the action of wild yeasts and bacteria present therein. It is sometimes referred to as "stale ale," although this is a feature that is celebrated, rather than a criticism. This character is similar to that found in lambic beers, although because of the robust nature of the old ale at the start of the maturation process, this character is much less pronounced than in the relatively delicate (when young) lambic beers.

Barley wine is, as you would expect, a slightly stronger proposition. It is brewed strong and meant to be sipped and savored. Again, it is more of an indulgence suited to the colder nights, although it is also a great way of rounding off a meal; rather than reaching for the spirits or liqueurs, I enjoy strong barley wine served in a brandy snifter or an oversized wine glass. In fact, it seems almost a shame to wait for the meal to be over to break out the barley wine, as it is such a fantastic accompaniment to full-flavored cheeses.

Barley wine is often seen as the pinnacle of a brewery's output and also as a test of the skill of the brewer. Although these beers are technically ales, which have a relatively fast fermentation and production process, they may take many weeks to ferment, and then a further period of maturation at the brewery before they are released. The breweries really go to a lot of trouble to produce these beers, but the spectacular results are always worth the effort.

barley wine

Of course, it's not really wine, although various prohibitions in the United States insist that these beers be labeled "barleywine-style ale" to avoid any confusion. As a group, these beers are characterized by fairly high alcohol content and a full, fruity malt character, leavened to varying degrees by balancing hop bitterness.

Almost everything here will benefit from a period of storage, anything from a year for the lightest examples to at least five years for the strongest. It would be unwise to drink anything this strong without some food; I find these are excellent after-dinner beers or even served with the cheese course.

Stilton—king of English cheeses—and barley wine are a traditional pairing

✚ Fuller's Vintage Ale

Brewed slightly differently each year, and good for extended aging, this vintage (2008) presents a luxurious aroma of oranges, fruitcake, and sherry. The classic Fuller's gingerbread note is present on the tongue, with more orange, marzipan, and toffee, but hops dry the finish nicely.

Food match: a selection of mature cheeses, including blue Stilton and strong Cheddar
Country: England
ABV: 8.5%; Serving temp.: 50-55°

✚ Hogs Back A Over T

Not all barley wines are endlessly unfurling hymns to the brewer's art. This is a sturdy, unfussy example, copper-brown in color with a good malty aroma (ripe and dried fruits, caramel); a sweet, fruity palate (quite low carbonation); and a long finish with a little hop bitterness.
Country: England
ABV: 9%; Serving temp.: 50-55°

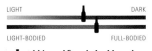

✚ Woodforde's Head Cracker

The tangy orange hop aroma on the nose suggests an IPA, but don't be fooled. The sweet, cough-drop edge to the palate and the persistently fruity finish (marmalade, bitter orange) are more in line with a barley wine. A sour plum note keeps it lively.
Country: England
ABV: 7%; Serving temp.: 50-55°

⊞ Nils Oscar Barley Wine

Dried fruit aromas (apricots, golden raisins) fill the glass above this copper-gold barley wine. Fruit on the palate (golden raisins again), with a hint of candy sugar, drying in the long finish. Where have they hidden the alcohol, you might ask? Give it 20 minutes, you'll find it.
Country: Sweden
ABV: 9.5%; Serving temp.: 50-55°

✚ JW Lees Moonraker

This ruddy-dark ale has a dense, creamy head and an aroma of dried fruits, sherry, and a hint of tartness that prevents it from seeming overly sweet. The palate is full-bodied and medium-sweet, with drying bitterness and a little tartness that carries into the long, fruity finish.
Country: England
ABV: 7.5%; Serving temp.: 50-55°

barley wine & old ale   223

O'Hanlons Thomas Hardy's Ale

Designed to be aged in the bottle. When young, it is intensely bittersweet, slightly burnt, and almost confrontational. With age, the flavors integrate and sherry, cognac, bitter oranges, and lashings of fruit slowly emerge. Can age for 25 years, but hits its stride, for me, at about 10 years old. Exceptional.

Food match: treat as an after-dinner liqueur, or serve with mature blue Stilton

Country: England
ABV: 11.7%; Serving temp.: 50-55°

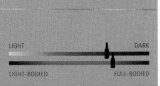

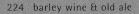

JW Lees Harvest Ale

"Brewed as a celebration of the brewer's art," it says on the label, and what a celebration it is. Malty dried fruit aromas pervade (fig, apricot, golden raisins), leading to a luscious, rich mouthful of sweet fruits and some spiciness. East Kent Goldings hops burst through the drying finish. A true classic.
Country: England
ABV: 11.5%; Serving temp.: 50-55°

Sierra Nevada Bigfoot

The hop aroma from this ruby-brown beer is frighteningly intense, but pucker up and enjoy it. Resinous hops awaken the nose, while on the tongue they counteract the malty sweetness, leaving a bittersweet aftertaste. Not for the fainthearted.
Country: USA
ABV: 9.6%; Serving temp.: 50-55°

Sharp's Massive Ale

Sharp's head brewer Stuart Howe showcases his skills here with an exceptional bottled barley wine. Massive Ale displays an enticing dried fruit nose with a touch of sherry, and plenty of raisin and prune flavors on the palate. The long, rich finish develops some autumnal spice notes. Very good indeed.
Country: England
ABV: 10%; Serving temp.: 50-55°

Flying Dog Horn Dog

There's a soft, fruity quality to this dark ruddy-brown beer that brings to mind butter-fried, sherry-soaked fruitcake. What do you mean, you don't fry fruitcake in butter? Get with it. Seriously, it's one of winter's great pleasures.
Country: USA
ABV: 10.2%; Serving temp.: 50-55°

Frederick, Maryland, home of the Flying Dog Brewery

old ale

Old ale is a very broad category, as the examples here demonstrate. Anchor Old Foghorn is a good beer to feature as a transition from barley wine to old ale, and it almost seems to embrace both categories simultaneously. Other examples here include beer with a notably aged bacterial influence, dark and smoky beers, and spiced ale. Though the variety is great, these beers are unified by having a hearty, robust quality, with the emphasis on malt character. They are the opposite of pale summer beers, suited to cold days, darker evenings, and moments of quiet contemplation.

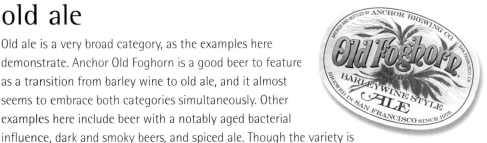

Adnams brew in Southwold, a small village on the East Anglian coast of England

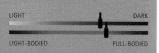 Anchor Brewing Old Foghorn

This is a five-star classic. Heady aromas of figs, cream sherry, cognac, and spice shimmer from the surface of this ruddy ale. There's a big burst of unctuous sweetness on the tongue, more figs, toasted bread, and then the trademark orangey bitterness pokes through the sweetish plummy finish. Excellent.

Food match: on its own, or with baked soft cheese scooped onto warm baguette
Country: USA
ABV: 8.8%; **Serving temp.:** 55°

LIGHT ——————— DARK
LIGHT-BODIED ——————— FULL-BODIED

✚ Woodforde's Norfolk Nog

This ruddy-dark is fabulously complex. There are notes of ripe banana skin, coffee, and licorice on the nose, and the palate bursts into life with bitter chocolate and a hint of smokiness. The finish is dry and lightly hopped, with more coffee and some dark berry fruit flavors.
Country: England
ABV: 4.6%; **Serving temp.:** 50–55°

LIGHT ——————— DARK
LIGHT-BODIED ——————— FULL-BODIED

✚ Box Steam Brewery Dark & Handsome

Can you have an old ale from a new brewery? This is a great beer. Ruddy-dark, with a pale tan head, and bursting with flavor—nuts, coffee, licorice, and dark berry fruits, wrapped up in a silky texture, finishing sweetish with roasty bitterness. Excellent.
Country: England
ABV: 5%; **Serving temp.:** 52–56°

LIGHT ——————— DARK
LIGHT-BODIED ——————— FULL-BODIED

✚ Theakstons Old Peculier

With its intentionally archaic spelling, this dark ruby ale is something of a classic. There is a soft malty edge to the aroma, leading with figs and licorice. In the mouth, chocolate and deeply roasted malt dominate the full-bodied palate, with more smoky licorice in the finish.
Country: England
ABV: 5.6%; **Serving temp.:** 55°

LIGHT ——————— DARK
LIGHT-BODIED ——————— FULL-BODIED

✚ Adnams Broadside

Something of an oddity, as the bottled beer is much stronger than the cask version. Bottled Broadside is a deep ruddy-brown, with a big fruitcake aroma and the right amount of dried fruit sweetness on the palate. The finish has a traditional English bitterness.
Country: England
ABV: 6.3%; **Serving temp.:** 50–55°

LIGHT ——————— DARK
LIGHT-BODIED ——————— FULL-BODIED

⊞ Greene King Strong Suffolk Vintage Ale

A blend of two beers—Best Pale Ale (5%abv) and Old 5X (15%abv). Besides its strength, Old 5X is notable for being matured in a huge oak vat. The resulting blend is mahogany brown and robustly fruity, with a slightly dry oaky tartness to the finish.

Food match: strong cheese and pickles are a perfect match, or hearty beef stew
Country: England
ABV: 6%; Serving temp.: 50-55°

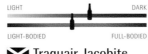

⊞ Dent T'owd Tup

The name translates from a Yorkshire dialect as "The Old Ram." Describing itself as "ruby red stout" on the label, but there is too much sweet fruitcake flavor for that. A ruby mild, then? Too much hop character. Delicious, complex, and as impenetrable as the dialect from which it is named.
Country: England
ABV: 6%; Serving temp.: 54°

LIGHT ──────── DARK
LIGHT-BODIED ──────── FULL-BODIED

✕ Traquair Jacobite Ale

A dark brown beer with ruby highlights. On top of the malty, woody aroma, there is a definite telltale sweetness of coriander spicing. This note carries into the sweetish palate (notes of vanilla cream and caramel) and persists into the long, drying finish.
Country: Scotland
ABV: 8%; Serving temp.: 55°

LIGHT ──────── DARK
LIGHT-BODIED ──────── FULL-BODIED

✕ Traquair House Ale

The complex aroma of this bronze-colored beer has a savory, almost meaty quality supporting the malt, plus hints of wood and butterscotch. The medium-weight palate manages to be malty and fairly dry at the same time. More wood is evident on the dry, persistent, and slightly resinous finish.
Country: Scotland
ABV: 7.2%; Serving temp.: 50-55°

LIGHT ──────── DARK
LIGHT-BODIED ──────── FULL-BODIED

⊞ Fuller's Gale's Prize Old Ale

Fullers' house yeast imparts a spicy gingerbread character to this classic old ale. Malt loaf on the nose, with an intentional hint of sourness livening up the palate. The sharpness recedes to a fruity finish, with lots of plum pudding and cognac character.
Country: England
ABV: 9%; Serving temp.: 50-55°

LIGHT ──────── DARK
LIGHT-BODIED ──────── FULL-BODIED

The interior of a traditional British pub

The Pike—a Brakspear's-branded pub in the picturesque Cotswolds hills, central England

✚ Marston's Owd Rodger

This mahogany-colored strong ale packs quite a punch, as suggested by the plums and fruitcake on the nose, and a faint whiff of alcohol. The palate is big and slightly sticky, with a little warmth on the swallow, and some hop dryness keeping the sweetness in check.

Food match: braised beef, blue cheese-stuffed mushrooms
Country: England
ABV: 7.6%; Serving temp.: 50–55°

✚ Robinson's Old Tom

The beguiling ruby highlights in this dark brown beer are just the start. The wonderful dried fruit malt aromas have a dark berry fruit edge, and the soft sweetness on the tongue is a joy. Some gentle bitterness emerges in the finish, but malt mostly dominates. Excellent with strong blue cheese.
Country: England
ABV: 8.5%; Serving temp.: 50–55°

✚ Brakspear Triple

This thrice-fermented, thrice-hopped beer is not your run-of-the-mill English ale. Aromatic hops and banana esters dominate the nose. The palate, though initially sweet, becomes dry, spicy, and nutty after the swallow. The alcohol is barely perceptible and very drinkable.
Country: England
ABV: 7.2%; Serving temp.: 50–55°

✚ Moorhouse's English Owd Ale

Old ales needn't necessarily be dark or terribly strong, as this fine example demonstrates. Peachy malt and toasted oats fill the aroma. The palate to this copper-gold ale is medium-sweet with a heady apricot finish. Only available as an export to the US.
Country: England
ABV: 5.9%; Serving temp.: 50–55°

⛉ Cooper's Dark

This ruddy-dark ale has a surprisingly full aroma, with coffee, licorice, and a little spice, while the fairly light body has a dry, nutty edge. More coffee, chocolate, and a faint woodiness appear in the finish. A very drinkable, light-bodied dark ale.
Country: Australia
ABV: 4.5%; Serving temp.: 50–55°

barley wine & old ale   231

porter & stout

Everyone can pick out a stout in a line of beers—it's the black one, usually with a creamy nitrogenated head sitting on top. Stout gets its color from the use of heavily roasted malt, and often from roasted raw barley, which adds a fresh-roasted quality to the brew. There's no question that Guinness is almost synonymous with stout—in fact, it may be the most widely recognized beer in the world—but there is a whole world of flavor beyond the classic pint of foaming black stuff.

Although porter is a style that has fallen from popularity, at one time it was quite the thing to drink. In London at the end of the eighteenth century, porter production was in its heyday, and the dark brown beer was everywhere. That's what porter was—a medium-strength dark brown ale, which (for preference) might have a few months' barrel aging to it, adding a hint of the sort of complexity that we've noted in lambic beers and "stale" old ales. Such was the taste for aged porter that breweries built large vats in which to age the beer before release. The largest of these, at the Meux Brewery in London, held around 150,000 gallons of beer. That much beer weighs quite a bit, and unsurprisingly the vat eventually gave way, giving rise to the great London porter flood of 1814, in which eight people died. That put an end to the fad of building huge aging vats.

Of course in brewing, nothing stays the same for very long. Brewers love to tinker with recipes, and eventually a stronger style of porter was produced. At the time, it was referred to as "stout porter," with "stout" meaning "strong" in the language of the day. Eventually, the reference to porter was dropped, and so stout was born. The irony is that over time, many stouts have become less strong and porter has gained an stronger "imperial" interpretation, with some examples reaching the low teens of alcohol content by volume. I'm not sure there is any style that is harder to unravel and understand than stout and porter.

There are some fairly monumental beers over the coming pages, but an equally good number of modest strength and exceptional balance. The black stuff looks a bit forbidding, but fear not—there are great depths of flavor to be enjoyed. Sure, it's an adult pleasure (all beer is), but if you can enjoy dark chocolate and coffee, then you have a palate that is ready to experience the delights of stout and porter.

porter

Although we now know that stout and porter are two sides
of the same coin, nothing is cast in stone. The porters listed in
these spreads just about manage to convey the style as being a lighter
stout, although some (notably Anchor Brewing, Saku, and Nøgne Ø) blur even those
faint dividing lines. Personally, I like a slight touch of sourness in a porter. I like to think
that a little tartness harks back to the days when porter would be stored in huge wooden
vats, something that surely couldn't be accomplished without a little bit of bacterial
influence adding some unusual character.

Different degrees of roasting affect the color and flavor of barley malts

⊞ Meantime London Porter

Alongside the expected notes of coffee and chocolate in this almost pitch-black beer, there is a smidgeon of stewed prune and even a hint of cola. The silky, rounded palate has a good roasted barley character, with a little sweetness, before finishing smoky, dry, and long.

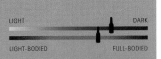

Food match: alternate fresh oysters with slices of spicy pork sausage
Country: England
ABV: 6.5%; Serving temp.: 50–55°

⊞ Cropton Blackout Porter

There is a huge creamy vanilla aroma to this ruby porter, along with a faint smokiness. The addition of unfermentable lactose (a natural "milk sugar") gives a surprising sweetness on the tongue, which is followed by a dry, slightly sour, vinous finish. Eccentric, but very enjoyable.
Country: England
ABV: 5%; Serving temp.: 52–58°

▬ Saku Porter

Soft roast malt notes (coffee, cocoa, and chocolate) pervade the aroma and palate, and last well into the fairly long smoky, earthy finish. Full-flavored enough to be enjoyable and satisfying, but complex and delicate enough to be very drinkable. A winter classic.
Country: Estonia
ABV: 7.5%; Serving temp.: 53–57°

▬ Svyturys-Utenos Porteris

There's a big, sweet-smelling aroma of banana and toffee to this ruddy-orange beer, and these flavors pop up prominently on the palate too. Full-bodied, quite sweet, with a little scorched caramel note bringing dryness to the finish. Unusual, but enjoyably chunky.
Country: Lithuania
ABV: 6.8%; Serving temp.: 45–50°

⊞ Naylor's Pinnacle Porter

The unusual fruity hop note (dark berries) on the nose of this dark brown porter combines well with the roasted grain aroma. A burst of fruitiness mid-palate (more dark fruit) leaves a fairly tart, dry finish, with a hint of sherbet. Unusual, but good drinking.
Country: England
ABV: 4.8%; Serving temp.: 50–55°

🏴󠁧󠁢󠁥󠁮󠁧󠁿 Burton Bridge Brewery Porter

There's a quality to the complex aroma of this ruddy porter—old wooden barrels, apples, plums, and oranges—that puts me in mind of a sherry bodega. The slight sweetness mid-palate dries fairly quickly, leaving an impression of unripe plums and tobacco. A lovely example of the style.

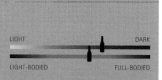

Food match: mixed platter of cheese and deli meats, or cold meat pie
Country: England
ABV: 4.5%; Serving temp.: 55°

✚ Bateman Salem Porter

Pouring almost as black as a stout, this ruby beer has a lovely aroma of chocolate malt, red fruits, and a little smokiness. After an initial exuberant blast of chocolate on the tongue, more fruit flits across the palate before a dry, roasty, and faintly tart finish.
Country: England
ABV: 4.7%; Serving temp.: 55–60°

🇩🇰 Carlsberg Carnegie Stark Porter

The roasted grain aroma has notes of coffee, dark fruit (prune, raisin), and a cognac-like, slightly perfumed note. Silky and smooth on the palate. Chocolate liqueur and stewed figs in the light but persistent finish. Great example of the Baltic style of porter—full-bodied but very drinkable.
Country: Denmark
ABV: 5.5%; Serving temp.: 50–55°

✚ Nethergate Old Growler

Famed for reviving traditional recipes, Nethergate Brewery recreated this recipe from the 1750s. There is a slightly charred, savory quality to the aroma along with plum and prune notes. Fairly light on the tongue with a fruity and slightly medicinal quality to the finish.
Country: England
ABV: 5.5%; Serving temp.: 50–55°

🇺🇸 Deschutes Black Butte Porter

Pouring dark brown, almost opaque, there are notes of smoky coffee and chocolate on the nose. The palate has an enjoyably creamy texture, with some dark berry fruit. The creaminess carries into the finish, which has more ripe, dark fruit and a smooth milk chocolate quality.
Country: USA
ABV: 5.2%; Serving temp.: 45–50°

Hearty meat pies are a great match for traditional porter

Ballast Point Brewery is named after the spot on Point Loma, near San Diego, where the first European expedition to explore California dropped anchor

🇺🇸 Ballast Point Black Marlin Porter

The trademark American craft brewers' love for hops with everything is apparent on the nose of this dark brown beer. Floral and citrus aromas jostle for space alongside licorice, mocha, and dark berry fruits. A deep, roasted bitterness comes through in the medium-dry finish.

Food match: Mexican mole, Moroccan-spiced lamb, barbecued ribs
Country: USA
ABV: 5.9%; Serving temp.: 50-55°

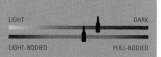

🇺🇸 Anchor Brewing Porter

This alluringly dark porter is almost opaque. If you can get any light to pass through it, there are ruby highlights. A big cappuccino-like head traps aromas of mocha, marzipan, smoke, and spice. On the palate, the creamy sweetness gives way to a lovely bitter chocolate finish.
Country: USA
ABV: 5.6%; Serving temp.: 50-55°

LIGHT · DARK
LIGHT-BODIED · FULL-BODIED

🇺🇸 Sierra Nevada Porter

There is a rounded aroma of roast grain and hops to this dark brown porter, along with a faint whiff of sourness. A little fruity sweetness on the palate gives way to a faintly sour, vinous quality on the swallow and a fairly long finish, with grassy hops and chocolate malt nicely in balance.
Country: USA
ABV: 5.6%; Serving temp.: 50-55°

LIGHT · DARK
LIGHT-BODIED · FULL-BODIED

🇳🇴 Nøgne Ø Porter

Porter is a style that evokes debate about authenticity, and although this is a great beer, it doesn't help the debate much. Pitch black, with a cappuccino head and an aroma of espresso and ripe dark fruits. The palate is hugely velvety, with a long bitter chocolate finish and some berry fruit.
Country: Norway
ABV: 7%; Serving temp.: 50-55°

LIGHT · DARK
LIGHT-BODIED · FULL-BODIED

🇫🇮 Panimoravintola Huvila Porter

Pouring almost stout-black, there is a surprising roasted-coffee intensity to this porter, leavened by some dark berry fruit character. Full-flavored and finishing dry and long, this beer can develop an enjoyably tart complexity after a few years in the bottle. Very nice indeed.
Country: Finland
ABV: 5.5%; Serving temp.: 50-55°

LIGHT · DARK
LIGHT-BODIED · FULL-BODIED

imperial porter

Oh dear. "Imperial porter" is one of those descriptions that can make a purist self-combust in an apoplectic fury. If you accept that stout is the heavier interpretation of porter, then imperial porter is de facto a stout. It's a good thing De Molen's beer is so delicious—that cuts through any argument. Port Brewing declines to define a style for Old Viscosity—I'm nailing my colors to the mast here and pronouncing it most at home in the company of porters, imperial or not. Flying Dog's well-hopped example is unconventional, but in this most disputed of styles, all the more fun for it.

Fried banana and vanilla ice cream go perfectly with imperial porter

🏴 De Molen Tsarina Esra Imperial Porter

Tar black and slightly thick, with a heady aroma of espresso, overripe banana, vanilla, and a slightly meaty note. The palate is intense, but not over-powering, with a smooth, slightly creamy coffee finish. Plenty of bitterness (hops and burnt malt) erupts after the swallow. Persistent, penetrating, but above all, balanced. Splendid.

Food match: it's vanilla ice cream and fried banana or nothing, I'm afraid
Country: Holland
ABV: 11%; Serving temp.: 50–55°

LIGHT ———————————— DARK

LIGHT-BODIED ———————— FULL-BODIED

🇺🇸 Port Brewing Old Viscosity

Deeply roasted (even burnt) malt, some burnt currant notes, and a very faint resinous hop aroma (orange, spice). The burnt notes carry into the palate, and the fiery theme is reinforced with a warm, glowing sensation after the swallow. Long, medium-dry finish with coffee, chocolate, and dried fruit. Intense.
Country: USA
ABV: 10%; Serving temp.: 55–60°

LIGHT ———————————— DARK

LIGHT-BODIED ———————— FULL-BODIED

🇺🇸 Flying Dog Gonzo Imperial Porter

Light, zesty, floral hop aromas sit atop a brooding, earthy, roasted malt quality. The palate is similarly divided—initially sweet, then a burst of aromatic hops, followed by a bitter, roasted malt note that sweeps across the palate like an approaching eclipse. Slightly eccentric, but good fun.
Country: USA
ABV: 8.7%; Serving temp.: 50–55°

LIGHT ———————————— DARK

LIGHT-BODIED ———————— FULL-BODIED

🇳🇴 Haandbryggeriet Porter

I'm not one for slavishly adhering to guidelines, but calling this a porter is misleading—it's more in the imperial stout mold. Pitch black and viscous, with a tan head and a deep chocolate aroma. Velvety texture, smooth, rich, roasty, earthy, smoky, and worryingly drinkable. Very good.
Country: Norway
ABV: 6.5%; Serving temp.: 50–55°

LIGHT ———————————— DARK

LIGHT-BODIED ———————— FULL-BODIED

🏴󠁧󠁢󠁳󠁣󠁴󠁿 Highland Brewing Orkney Porter

Dark mahogany with ruby highlights, this porter has a lovely roasted grain aroma and dark berry fruit. After a slight tartness (always a good sign in a porter), coffee and chocolate dominate the palate, with a hint of smoke lending complexity. Nutty chocolate pervades the finish.
Country: Scotland
ABV: 9%; Serving temp.: 52–58°

LIGHT ———————————— DARK

LIGHT-BODIED ———————— FULL-BODIED

smoked porter

This is a category of beer that tends to separate the dedicated beer-hound from the merely curious. Not that there is anything terribly challenging about the beers listed here, but for some reason, the addition of a little smoked malt seems to be a step too far for some. The three listed here are all beautifully balanced. The two unsmoked beers here are pretty fine too—special mention to Saltaire Brewery for taking a pet peeve of mine, flavored beer, and making something so balanced and downright drinkable that even I find myself enjoying it.

Oysters are a good food match for smoked porter

➕ Okells Smoked Porter

It's just about possible to discern the smoked malt in the aroma of this dark brown porter, alongside hints of chocolate, vanilla, and coffee. The smoke moves a little more to the fore on the palate, but nicely in balance, supporting and adding interest to the dry, phenolic finish.

Food match: seafood—fresh oysters, smoked mackerel, fruits de mer
Country: England
ABV: 4.7%; Serving temp.: 50–55°

LIGHT   DARK

LIGHT-BODIED   FULL-BODIED

▥ Nils Oscar Rökporter

There's no mistaking the smoky aroma that leaps from this dark ruddy-brown beer, but there is also a soft creamy fruitiness woven in as well. The palate is smoky but well-integrated, with the dark fruit, bitter coffee, and rich creamy smoothness of the porter showing through. Beautifully balanced.
Country: Sweden
ABV: 6%; Serving temp.: 52–58°

LIGHT   DARK

LIGHT-BODIED   FULL-BODIED

➕ Saltaire Hazelnut Coffee Porter

This glowing red ale is a real treat. The aroma is a burst of red berry fruit, nuts, coffee, and Goldings hops. The silky texture (oats) delivers the fleeting impression of hazelnut coffee, while the medium-dry finish dries to floral hoppiness. Unexpectedly enjoyable.
Country: England
ABV: 4.6%; Serving temp.: 54°

LIGHT   DARK

LIGHT-BODIED   FULL-BODIED

➕ Kelham Island Brooklyn Smoked Porter

A collaboration between the Brooklyn and Kelham Island Breweries, this was a one-off cultural exchange that has thankfully made it into more regular production. The soft, smoky aroma and palate have notes of licorice and mocha. The smokiness is enjoyably complex.
Country: England
ABV: 6.5%; Serving temp.: 52–58°

LIGHT   DARK

LIGHT-BODIED   FULL-BODIED

➕ Samuel Smith's Taddy Porter

There is a lovely honeyed nuttiness on the nose of this dark porter, along with some deeply roasted grain smokiness. The beer initially appears sweet, with a little fruitiness, but the roasted grain lends a bitter dryness to the finish, although some fruitiness persists.
Country: England
ABV: 5%; Serving temp.: 55°

LIGHT   DARK

LIGHT-BODIED   FULL-BODIED

porter & stout   243

imperial stout

Imperial Russian stout—now there's a phrase that evokes a time and place in history. Thick black stout, shipped from England to the Russian Steppes by Albert Le Coq, a legendary Belgian merchant whose name has become synonymous with the most complex, vinous, and intense stout that money can buy. This intensity can only be matched with the sort of bourbon barrel-aged offering that Goose Island offers here. While bigger is usually better, there are also some understated classics here too—Sam Smith's version has been a touchstone of the style for many American craft brewers.

The Anchor Tavern at 34 Park Street, Southwark, London. This pub was associated with Thrale's, who made the very first imperial stout, and was once frequented by London's leading writers and actors.

 Goose Island Bourbon County Brand Stout

This beer is big, but it has grace as well. The huge aroma of coffee, chocolate, and bourbon makes you think that you are going to get knocked flat, but no. Flavors of coffee, nuts, chocolate, vanilla, smoke, leather, and prunes jostle each other but manage to remain harmonious. Beautiful.

Food match: chocolate truffles, crème brûlée, or as an ice cream float shot
Country: USA
ABV: 13%; Serving temp.: 53–57°

Thornbridge St. Petersburg Imperial Russian Stout

A brooding and opaque imperial stout with an atypical fruitiness. The burst of fruits on the palate suggests some interesting hopping, with red and black currants, before the rich, slightly oily coffee and chocolate notes on the palate dominate.
Country: England
ABV: 7.7%; Serving temp.: 50–55°

Nils Oscar Imperial Stout

Although light-bodied for an imperial stout, it's still as black as the inside of a closet at midnight. Coffee, roasted malt, and, improbably, smoked almonds on the nose. The palate is quite light, medium-dry, with a creamy taste and texture. Surprisingly delicate for the style.
Country: Sweden
ABV: 7%; Serving temp.: 50–55°

Samuel Smith's Imperial Stout

A fruity, almost vinous aroma to this none-more-black imperial stout lies delicately atop the vigorous hurly-burly of espresso, burnt currants, and bitter chocolate. From the silky entrance to the bittersweet finish, this is an acknowledged classic of the style.
Country: England
ABV: 7%; Serving temp.: 60°

Alvinne Podge Belgian Imperial Stout

Commissioned by Chris Pollard of Podge's Belgian Beer tours ("Driving People to Drink Since 1994"), this is a surprisingly lithe imperial stout. The nose has plenty of fruit (pears, bananas, some citrus), while the palate is dry. Sour plums and bitter chocolate emerge in the finish.
Country: Belgium
ABV: 10.5%; Serving temp.: 50–55°

porter & stout   245

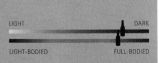 Harvey's Le Coq Imperial Extra Double Stout

Black as tar and only slightly more runny, this gives off an intense aroma of dried fruit, smoke, burnt currants, figs, prunes, sherry, and winter spice. Unctuous, giving a hit of sherry followed by bitter espresso, soy, and cognac. Meaty, vinous, empyreumatic, and very grown-up, a bittersweet-savory anachronism. Splendid.

Food match: panna cotta with raspberry coulis, red fruit cheesecake, or great on its own
Country: England
ABV: 9%; Serving temp.: 50-55°

LIGHT ———————— DARK

LIGHT-BODIED ———— FULL-BODIED

Brooklyn Black Chocolate Stout

This pitch-black, velvety stout is another notch on brewmaster Garret Oliver's brewing paddle. Slightly viscous on the pour, the huge aroma of dark chocolate and espresso is apparent even at arm's length. Initially sweet, with a persistent bitter chocolate note emerging in the finish. Luscious.
Country: USA
ABV: 10.6%; Serving temp.: 55°

LIGHT ———————— DARK

LIGHT-BODIED ———— FULL-BODIED

BrewDog Paradox Imperial Stout

Paradox is a collection of imperial stouts aged in different whiskey casks. It sounds simple, but the whiskey has a huge influence on the flavor, giving anything from a peaty, phenolic blast to a rounded, spicy sweetness. Something for everyone, then, except the fainthearted.
Country: Scotland
ABV: 10%; Serving temp.: 52-58°

LIGHT ———————— DARK

LIGHT-BODIED ———— FULL-BODIED

Stone Imperial Russian Stout

Blacker than Satan's heart, with appropriate accompanying burnt aromas—espresso, boiling tar, charcoal, a little peat smoke, and a spirity note. Unctuous on the palate, with more espresso, Islay whisky, dried (and burnt) fruit, and some port wine character. Intense, bittersweet, and supernaturally persistent.
Country: USA
ABV: 10.8%; Serving temp.: 50-55°

LIGHT ———————— DARK

LIGHT-BODIED ———— FULL-BODIED

Great Divide Yeti Imperial Stout

Looking terrifyingly like dark matter as it glops from the bottle, this pitch-dark stout has a big aroma of creamy cappuccino, vanilla, and pine needles. If that sounds unnerving, don't be put off, as the riot of bitter chocolate, fruit, and winter spices is worth surrendering yourself to.
Country: USA
ABV: 9.5%; Serving temp.: 50-55°

LIGHT ———————— DARK

LIGHT-BODIED ———— FULL-BODIED

Chocolate malt, shown here, adds a deep nutty flavor to stouts and porters

Beer and caviar sounds like an odd match—but it can work, if the beer you choose is a suitably sophisticated one

 BrewDog Rip Tide Stout

The bottle states "Serving Suggestion: pour into a glass and enjoy with an air of aristocratic nonchalance." They're right; wearing a cravat does give this beer a rakish edge. Espresso, fruitcake, and cognac stage an almighty ruckus, while the intense mocha and dried fruit palate eventually comes to a faintly sour finish.

Food match: follow the Tsars—caviar, smoked salmon, and sour cream
Country: Scotland
ABV: 8%; Serving temp.: 50–55°

LIGHT ——————— DARK

LIGHT-BODIED ——————— FULL-BODIED

 Lion Lion Stout

This beer makes no claim to be an imperial stout (rather than an "ordinary"), but its intensity is in imperial territory. Deep-roasted mocha aromas and a little toffee on the nose; sweet coffee, vanilla, and a little dried plum on the palate. Long, bittersweet mocha finish. Great.
Country: Sri Lanka
ABV: 8%; Serving temp.: 55°

LIGHT ——————— DARK

LIGHT-BODIED ——————— FULL-BODIED

 De Dolle Brouwers Extra Stout

Black, with a tan head, and a powerful aroma of dried and burned currants on a fruitcake. Palate is huge, sweet, although just about balanced. Long, fruity, and burnt-bitter finish. Over time, this beer gains a splendid, heady, almost vinous complexity. One for the cellar, methinks.
Country: Belgium
ABV: 9%; Serving temp.: 48–52°

LIGHT ——————— DARK

LIGHT-BODIED ——————— FULL-BODIED

 Nøgne Ø Imperial Stout

An opaque, ink-black imperial stout, with a huge aroma of espresso, dark chocolate, heavily roasted grain, and a slightly heady alcohol hit. The palate is unctuous, initially sweet with some dried fruit and vanilla notes, but becomes bitter in the finish, with some resinous hop character.
Country: Norway
ABV: 9%; Serving temp.: 48–52°

LIGHT ——————— DARK

LIGHT-BODIED ——————— FULL-BODIED

 Ellezelloise Hercule Stout

There are a few exceptions that prove the rule, but stouts aren't really a Belgian thing. Discovering this tarry, pitch-black monster, then, was a revelation. Slightly thick, with a tan head, this chewy stout has a deep, bitter richness that almost qualifies it as an imperial. Worth seeking out.
Country: Belgium
ABV: 9%; Serving temp.: 50–55°

LIGHT ——————— DARK

LIGHT-BODIED ——————— FULL-BODIED

stout

Stout is one of those styles that everyone seems to recognize, but oddly that familiarity doesn't translate into lots of people drinking it. I suppose there is something forbidding about a glass of black beer (white foamy head optional), but unlike the imperial stouts in the previous section, these stouts are nothing to be wary of—they mostly offer no more threat to the palate than a cup of black coffee, and have a similar sort of taste. And mostly, they offer a wonderful amount of flavor and depth for a relatively modest alcohol content.

Mushroom risotto prepared with fresh porcini. Creamy foods pair surprisingly well with stout.

Cooper's Best Extra Stout

Although it has always been a good example, this stout appears to have gotten better of late. There is an appealing, slightly wild note in the nose, while the medium-bodied palate has a good, solid, roasted barley bitterness and a nutty finish. Bottle-conditioning undoubtedly adds to the complexity.

Food match: fresh oysters, wild mushroom risotto
Country: Australia
ABV: 6.3%; Serving temp.: 50-55°

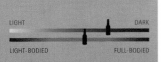

Guinness Special Export

There isn't huge aroma to this ink-black beer; a little roast grain, perhaps some leafy bittering hops. So it's all the more surprising when it leaps onto the palate shouting "TA-DAH!" and leaves flavors of espresso, dark chocolate, licorice, and ripe dark berries in its wake.
Country: Ireland
ABV: 8%; Serving temp.: 50-55°

Sierra Nevada Stout

Deeply roasted grain with a slightly husky edge is the dominant aroma here. The palate has a full-bodied creamy richness to it, and there is a little trademark sweetness mid-palate. The finish develops a soft espresso note, along with some drying hoppiness.
Country: USA
ABV: 5.8%; Serving temp.: 45-50°

Hambleton Nightmare Stout

The label on bottles of this ruddy stout talks about "the roasted barley rearing out of the four malt brew," and they're not kidding. The prominent roasted grain flavors harmonize well on the palate, with a sweetish coffee note, before a relatively light, dry, and bitter finish.
Country: England
ABV: 5%; Serving temp.: 50-55°

Ridgeway Foreign Export Stout

"Satisfyingly foreign," the back label of this jet-black stout cryptically proclaims. The spicy aroma has coffee, caramel, and custard notes, hinting at its strength. On the palate, coffee, licorice, and dried fruit dominate, before a persistent hoppy finish and warming alcohol kick.
Country: England
ABV: 8%; Serving temp.: 50-55°

⊕ Hook Norton Double Stout

It's hard to pinpoint exactly why this stout is so enjoyable. To describe it is to run through the litany of classic stout aromas (dried fruit, coffee, chocolate) and flavors (cocoa, dark caramel, faintly smoky), and yet that doesn't really do it justice. Much greater than the sum of its parts.

Food match: grilled steak, steak and oyster pie
Country: England
ABV: 4.8%; Serving temp.: 50-55°

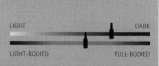

LIGHT — DARK

LIGHT-BODIED — FULL-BODIED

⊕ Hop Back Entire Stout

There is a nice, balanced drinkability to this medium-bodied stout. The aroma has a pleasant milk chocolate quality, with some light red fruitiness. The lovely silky texture gives way to a lightly bitter coffee-and-cream flavor, with coffee and red fruits returning in the finish.
Country: England
ABV: 4.5%; Serving temp.: 50-55°

LIGHT — DARK

LIGHT-BODIED — FULL-BODIED

≣ Deschutes Obsidian Stout

Obsidian is a black volcanic glass, and you can see the similarity when you pour this brilliant but impenetrably black stout. There is a creaminess that seems to be a characteristic of Deschutes' darker beers (a result of the *krausen*?), with lots of dark fruit and strong coffee flavors.
Country: USA
ABV: 6.4%; Serving temp.: 50-55°

LIGHT — DARK

LIGHT-BODIED — FULL-BODIED

⊕ Burton Bridge Brewery Bramble Stout

Clearly something fruity is going on in this medium-bodied stout. On top of the house style, with its almost sherryish complexity, the addition of blackberries gives a subtle earthy sweetness to the palate. Finish is dry, slightly vinous, with an almost savory tang.
Country: England
ABV: 5%; Serving temp.: 50-55°

LIGHT — DARK

LIGHT-BODIED — FULL-BODIED

⊕ St Peter's Cream Stout

St Peter's have done a great job of building an iconic beer brand without dumbing down their beers. This is a beauty, with a mouthwatering aroma of roasted grain, dried fruit and a creamy note. Full and slightly sweet on the palate, with a roasted, creamy and pleasantly bitter finish.
Country: England
ABV: 6.5%; Serving temp.: 50-55°

LIGHT — DARK

LIGHT-BODIED — FULL-BODIED

Steak is a traditional pie filling that can pair well with a creamy Irish stout. Sometimes, as here, the stout can also feature in the pie filling.

flavored stout

The stouts in this section are distinguished by having an unusual ingredient added to the brew. There's nothing too outlandish here, just an extra flavor component that enhances stout's given character. Unsurprisingly, coffee and chocolate are popular additions. Sadly, I was unable to track down an odd-sounding peppermint stout—it sounds like the kind of thing that you either love or hate, and I'm afraid to say that I might not have tasted it with a completely open mind. Flavored beers really aren't my thing, but I happily exempt all of the stouts here.

Coffee beans add a slightly bitter, roasted note when used to flavor stout

O'Hanlons Port Stout

The nose of this medium-bodied stout has a lively red currant fruitiness, alongside the more conventional aromas of coffee and cocoa, no doubt the result of it being enriched with ruby port. The palate and finish have a ripe berry quality, adding a little lift to an already good stout.

Food match: anchovy and garlic-stuffed roast lamb, with red currant sauce
Country: England
ABV: 4.8%; Serving temp.: 50–55°

Ossett Treacle Stout

Molasses gives this mahogany stout a cough-drop aroma. The palate is fairly dry, with a certain smokiness that gives the impression of burnt toffee. A nicely rounded coffee-and-cola finish, with some persistent, perfumed hop notes.
Country: England
ABV: 5%; Serving temp.: 52–58°

LIGHT — DARK
LIGHT-BODIED — FULL-BODIED

Mikkeller Beer Geek Breakfast Pooh Coffee Cask Festival Edition

This rich, intense stout, with an assertive fresh hop presence, was brewed specially with civet-passed coffee beans for the 2008 European Beer Festival in Copenhagen. Mikkeller's Beer Geek Breakfast "Weasel" is a more easily found version.
Country: Denmark
ABV: 7%; Serving temp.: 50–55°

LIGHT — DARK
LIGHT-BODIED — FULL-BODIED

Dark Star Espresso Stout

Pitch black (but relatively light-bodied), this stout has a smoky and slightly burnt aroma, similar to fresh heavy-roasted coffee beans. The palate is fairly light but manages to cram in lots of bitter chocolate and espresso flavor (espresso beans are added to the brew kettle). Dry finish.
Country: England
ABV: 4.2%; Serving temp.: 50–55°

LIGHT — DARK
LIGHT-BODIED — FULL-BODIED

Wells & Youngs Young's Double Chocolate Stout

This stout always surprises new drinkers with its accessibility. Dark brown, with ruby highlights and a tan head, it has a roasted coffee note with some milk chocolate aroma. The palate is drier than expected and has a balanced, chocolate-accented finish.
Country: England
ABV: 5.2%; Serving temp.: 55°

LIGHT — DARK
LIGHT-BODIED — FULL-BODIED

oatmeal stout

To the uninitiated, oatmeal stout sounds like it might be
the worst of many worlds—a glass of lumpy black liquid.
However, the proportion of oatmeal in a brew is very low,
and although it influences the flavor a little, adding a
creamy edge, the principal benefit it confers is in the texture.
Oatmeal stouts have a lovely silky quality to them, most evident as the first sip
hits the tongue, but present throughout. Dragon Stout uses no oatmeal but is a relic of
an unusual (and rarely seen) style, sweet stout. And you can't talk about stout without
mentioning classic draft Guinness.

**A recreation of a traditional cooperage at the Guinness Brewery shows how wooden stout
casks were made**

 Samuel Smith's Oatmeal Stout

It's all here, from the trademark malty nuttiness (or is it a nutty maltiness?) to the lingering, bittersweet finish. In between, we have a lovely silky texture (from the oatmeal), a coffee liqueur center, and a roasted barley bitterness that builds to leave a balanced finish.

Food match: brown bread with good butter and French and English cheeses
Country: England
ABV: 5%; Serving temp.: 55°

 Bridge Of Allan Glencoe Wild Oat Stout

This modestly strong beer has a surprising amount of complexity. Some dark berry fruitiness on the nose, alongside coffee and a little smokiness. The palate is a little thin, but the burst of flavor on the swallow compensates—dark fruit, coffee, and peat smoke. Lovely.
Country: Scotland
ABV: 4.5%; Serving temp.: 58-62°

Guinness Draught

The creamy white nitrogenated head atop a pitch black beer looks forbidding, but don't be put off. The texture is silky and surprisingly smooth, and the flavor is of roasted barley (think weak coffee) rather than anything too intense and bitter. A global icon, available everywhere, for a reasonable price.
Country: Ireland
ABV: 4.1%; Serving temp.: 45-50°

 Wensleydale Black Dub

Where to start with this lovely stout? The creamy oats are fairly prominent in the aroma, alongside a smoky, roasted note and a faintly vinous quality. It glides across the tongue like satin, leaving flavors of dark berries, chocolate, and bittersweet coffee.
Country: England
ABV: 4.4%; Serving temp.: 52-57°

Desnoes & Geddes Dragon Stout

Sweet stout used to be a relatively common style but is now quite hard to find. This is dark ruddy-brown, with an aroma of roasted and scorched malt, and some fruitiness (cherries?). The palate is quite sweet and silky (lactose?), with little bitterness, but a slight tartness in the finish.
Country: Jamaica
ABV: 7.5%; Serving temp.: 50-55°

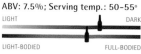

porter & stout   257

oddities, rarities & specialties

There's no getting away from it—this chapter is full of beers that struggle to fit in anywhere else. The world of brewing is inhabited by real people, and like real people everywhere, this means that eccentricities are bound to manifest themselves. We kick off with some German regional specialties, which, although they look like lagers and receive a similar long period of cold maturation to a classic pilsner, are actually brewed with top-fermenting yeast. This imparts a very slight fruitiness that is absent in pilsner, but makes both kölsch and altbier something special.

The barrel-aged beers that follow are a throwback to a bygone age when all beer was served from the wood. Although older, well-used barrels don't contribute any character to the beer (and many used to be lined with pitch to make sure this was the case), these beers have been aged in old whiskey casks, which has given them an extra depth of flavor, strength, and a little wild complexity too.

The Christmas beers listed here have ended up being almost all Belgian. Although most breweries produce a seasonal special (and you should try to find out what your local brewery produces during the colder months—it will be something that they are proud of), the Belgians go at it with characteristic gusto, making beers that are particularly appropriate to the time of year. They are big beers, and if you drink them on their own, they will get you into trouble fast. However, savor them with a plate of seasonal treats, and they make a lot more sense (and do less damage).

Smoked beers are undoubtedly an acquired taste. In fact, the Heller-Trum Brewery suggests that you might have to drink up to ten glasses of it to get that taste—hopefully not at one sitting. Technically, these beers are lagers, but give these to someone who has only ever drunk lager (be it pilsner or a more commercial interpretation) and there will be puzzled looks. The originals are real "love it or hate it" beers, and although I struggled to enjoy them for a long time, I finally had my "Eureka!" moment drinking the Rauchbier Urbock on draft at a beer festival. It really was worth persevering for, although in total I think it took less than ten glasses over a few years.

If you haven't skipped to the end of the book yet, it might not surprise you to hear that's where the strongest and rarest beers have ended up. These aren't for the faint-hearted and are at the end for a reason—they are the final destination on a journey of beer appreciation that has been set out over the preceding pages. However far you manage to travel, I hope you enjoy the ride.

german regional specialties

The German brewing scene is highly regionalized, with very few national brands. These are not the only regional specialties you can find in Germany (for example, the smoked beers of southern Germany appear in their own "Smoked Beers" section), but they are relatively easy to find (if you visit the appropriate city) and closely linked to a sense of place. Kölsch is brewed in and around Cologne (Köln in German, hence kölsch) and is a delicate, fruity, golden lagerbier. The other side of the coin reveals the robust, brown Altbier of Düsseldorf and beyond—also a smooth lagerbier, but with more dark malt and bitter hop character.

Drinking beer outside in the Bavarian mountains

Sünner Kölsch

Trying to describe the delicate aromas and flavors of kölsch is like trying to catch fog; you wave your arms around but don't really get anywhere. Sünner has a softly perfumed quality to the aroma, a gentle malty fruitiness to the palate, and a very mild bitterness to the finish.

Food match: roast pork sandwiches (schweinbröt) and applesauce, delicate fish dishes
Country: Germany
ABV: 4.8%; Serving temp.: 48°

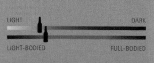

Dom Kölsch

In the very finely grouped world of kölsch, Dom seems to have a little something that sets it apart from the others. That's not to say that it's a radical departure, but Dom's kölsch does have a fresh, slightly sappy quality that seems to imbue it with a bit more life.
Country: Germany
ABV: 4.8%; Serving temp.: 48°

Gaffel Kölsch

There is a definite grassy hop aroma and pale malt note to this golden kölsch. Light, spritzy, and clean as a whistle on the palate, with a touch of cracker and hop bitterness in the aftertaste. One of the more assertive examples, but not by much.
Country: Germany
ABV: 4.8%; Serving temp.: 48°

Küppers Kölsch

It might be easier to describe the taste of a distinctive bottled water than to describe this refined example. There is a faint aroma of pine needles (or is it citrus, or both?) presumably from the hops, which reappears briefly in the incredibly clean, dry, and vaguely floral finish.
Country: Germany
ABV: 4.8%; Serving temp.: 48°

PJ Früh Kölsch

It's hard to explain why such a delicate beer is so enjoyable, but it is. A very refined malt aroma from this fresh, pale kölsch, with a hint of vanilla and lemon about it. On the soft, rounded palate, there is a light bitterness before leaving a gentle, lemony dryness.
Country: Germany
ABV: 4.8%; Serving temp.: 48°

Frankenheim Alt

There is something about the color of this beer (dark brown with coppery highlights) that hints at the intensity of flavor. The big, nutty malt aroma is faintly savory and has a suggestion of smokiness and spice (gingerbread) to it. The robust, hoppy palate finishes dry, bitter, and slightly herbal.

Food match: a traditional German sauerbraten
Country: Germany
ABV: 4.8%; Serving temp.: 48°

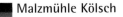

Malzmühle Kölsch

The clue is in the name, which translates as "malt mill." Accordingly, there is a pronounced pale malt character to this kölsch that seems to give it an almost creamy, mouth-filling texture and—I would, of course, never advocate beer as a meal substitute—an almost nourishing quality.
Country: Germany
ABV: 4.8%; Serving temp.: 48°

Bolten Alt

Medium-brown in color, this altbier has a slightly austere quality, but that's not to say it's flavorless. There is plenty of nutty malt and spicy hop to the nose and also on the palate, which is full-bodied with very little sweetness, becoming more dry in the finish.
Country: Germany
ABV: 4.9%; Serving temp.: 48–52°

Bolten Ur-Alt

If you upend the bottle before pouring, this unfiltered altbier is so cloudy that it almost looks like a dark wheat beer. However, the aroma has an austere hoppy and herbal edge (with some yeasty notes), and the palate, silky in texture, is pleasantly dry, nutty, and bitter.
Country: Germany
ABV: 4.8%; Serving temp.: 48°

Schlosser Alt

The slightly toffeeish note, produced by warmer, top-fermentation of medium-roast malt, is immediately evident on the nose of this altbier. The slightly sweet palate has a spicy note to it (gingerbread), and the finish has a dry, nutty quality, with a little bitterness emerging.
Country: Germany
ABV: 4.8%; Serving temp.: 48°

Hop-growing in Franconia, southern Germany

cask-aged beer

Like a lot of beer drinkers, I'm also fond of whiskey—they are made from the same ingredients (bar the hops) and brewed in the same way, although of course whiskey is distilled. The magic in a distillery happens in the cask—the wooden barrel that the spirit is aged in. Using old sherry or madeira barrels imparts a particularly rich flavor. So it is with beer—a period of time spent in an old whiskey barrel imparts smooth, rich character, and quite often a slightly wild edge too. Barrel-aging can't make a bad beer good, but it can make a good beer great.

Stacked wooden barrels in Andechs—a Bavarian monastery that has brewed beer since 1455

🏴󠁧󠁢󠁳󠁣󠁴󠁿 Harviestoun Ola Dubh 30yr Old

I always feel that if a beer has had some barrel aging, then it should emerge tasting plush and polished. This venerable beer has many layers of flavor—smoke, charred meat, sea spray, and tar, all topped off by a smooth, sweet, vanilla note of old oak barrels.

Food match: strong blue or smoked cheese, smoked fish, fresh seafood
Country: Scotland
ABV: 8%; Serving temp.: 50-55°

LIGHT ——————————————— DARK

LIGHT-BODIED ——————————— FULL-BODIED

🏴󠁧󠁢󠁳󠁣󠁴󠁿 Orkney Dark Island Reserve

Subtitled "The Extraordinary Orcadian Ale," this is finished in whiskey casks, giving the beer a luscious, burnished quality. There is dark fruit (both stewed and dried), winter spice, oak, and an almost savory base note. It's produced in very small batches, which tend to sell out quickly. Worth hunting down.
Country: Scotland
ABV: 10%; Serving temp.: 50-55°

LIGHT ——————————————— DARK

LIGHT-BODIED ——————————— FULL-BODIED

🏴󠁧󠁢󠁳󠁣󠁴󠁿 Harviestoun Ola Dubh 12yr Old

"Aged in selected oak casks used to mature Highland Park's beautifully balanced 12-Year-Old Single Malt Scotch Whisky," says the label. Old Engine Oil is transformed into a more complex creature—earthy and slightly meaty, with a tang of the sea. A very grown-up dark ale.
Country: Scotland
ABV: 8%; Serving temp.: 50-55°

LIGHT ——————————————— DARK

LIGHT-BODIED ——————————— FULL-BODIED

🏴󠁧󠁢󠁳󠁣󠁴󠁿 Bridge Of Allan Tullibardine 1488 Whisky Ale

Aged in casks from the Tullibardine Distillery, this copper-orange ale has had a lot of hop and malt, rich, creamy character derived from whiskey oak. Butterscotch, vanilla, coconut, toasted bread, and a long orange fruit finish.
Country: Scotland
ABV: 7%; Serving temp.: 50-55°

LIGHT ——————————————— DARK

LIGHT-BODIED ——————————— FULL-BODIED

➕ Fuller's Brewer's Reserve No. 1

Aged in 30-year-old malt whiskey casks for 500 days, there is a distinct "barrel flora" aroma to this beer. This adds an enjoyable complexity to the burnished bronze beer, which has a good hop character (bitter orange), coconut, vanilla, and a pleasantly bitter, almost tart finish.
Country: England
ABV: 7.7%; Serving temp.: 50-55°

LIGHT ——————————————— DARK

LIGHT-BODIED ——————————— FULL-BODIED

christmas beer

Although Christmas isn't the coldest time of year, it is a time for a bit of indulgence. Brewers have traditionally brewed "winter warmers," darker, stronger beers that offer a form of sustenance for both body (and soul) to see one through the long nights of midwinter. The beers here are predominantly from Belgium, because for me, no one does full-bodied, sweet, and strong beers like the Belgians. They also love a bit of cheesy snow-and-Santa-hat action on the label—if you're going to brew a strong Christmas beer, there's no place for subtlety.

Christmas in Brussels—a city which takes the holiday brewing very seriously

✠ Shepherd Neame Christmas Ale

Unlike many British brewers, Shepherd Neame has the courage to pump everything up a bit in its ruddy Christmas beer. The malt-driven sweetness is entirely appropriate, with some nice red fruit and plums in evidence. The higher alcohol provides a little warming glow, and some hop dryness appears later on.

Food match: a slice of fruitcake with a piece of medium-strong hard cheese
Country: England
ABV: 7%; Serving temp.: 50-55°

LIGHT ———————————— DARK
LIGHT-BODIED ———————————— FULL-BODIED

▮▮ John Martin Gordon Xmas

Mahogany in color with ruby highlights, this winter warmer has a massive fruity aroma—overripe banana, dates, figs, and brown sugar. An initial stickiness dries a little to a medium finish, with lashings of more bananas, dried fruit, and a burnt-sugar note. Very good in cold weather.
Country: Belgium
ABV: 8.8%; Serving temp.: 48-53°

LIGHT ———————————— DARK
LIGHT-BODIED ———————————— FULL-BODIED

▮▮ Du Bocq Corsendonk Christmas

Pouring a slightly cloudy brown color, the aroma is a riot of sweet chocolate malt and fruitcake. The chocolate note carries into the palate, and there is a hint of liqueur-soaked cherries or rumtopf in the finish, which has an enjoyable alcohol warmth. A lovely winter warmer.
Country: Belgium
ABV: 8.5%; Serving temp.: 48-53°

LIGHT ———————————— DARK

LIGHT-BODIED ———————————— FULL-BODIED

▮▮ De Dolle Brouwers Stille Nacht

A relatively pale copper color for a winter beer, but then what would you expect from the Mad Brewers ("De Dolle Brouwers")? A persistent creamy head traps aromas of winter spice, cream sherry, and dried apricots, while the lively palate starts out fruity before drying to a peppery finish.
Country: Belgium
ABV: 12%; Serving temp.: 48-53°

LIGHT ———————————— DARK

LIGHT-BODIED ———————————— FULL-BODIED

▮▮ Huyghe Delirium Noel

Despite being stronger and darker than its "Tremens" sibling, this Christmas special seems somehow more elegant. A ruby-colored beer, with a sweet winter spiciness and rich notes of plums and sweet liqueur-soaked cherries at its core.
Country: Belgium
ABV: 10%; Serving temp.: 48-53°

LIGHT ———————————— DARK

LIGHT-BODIED ———————————— FULL-BODIED

oddities, rarities & specialties   267

smoked beer

Rauchbier (literally "smoke beer") is a singular style, a throwback to an older era of malting and brewing. The smoked beers of the Heller-Trum Brewery are legendary. But they don't have a monopoly on smoked beers—there are others brewed all over the world, utilizing the heady, phenolic qualities of smoked malt to produce beers of varying degrees of smokiness. Used with restraint, as in the example from Meantime (and some of the smoked porters earlier in the book), it can add an extra layer of flavor and aroma that is perceived as being slightly savory.

Salted and cured meats such as corned beef are ideally served with smoked beers

▬▬ Heller-Trum Schlenkerla Rauchbier Urbock

While Schlenkerla Märzen has a dry austerity to it, the slightly darker Urbock is a much bigger-boned brew. The smokiness lends a lovely, savory quality to the beer, while the sweet malt poking through mid-palate gives a compelling drinkability. Finishes sweet and smoky. An exceptional beer.

Food match: predictably, cured and smoked meats, or broiled pork tenderloin
Country: Germany
ABV: 6.5%; Serving temp.: 48–52°

LIGHT ————————————— DARK

LIGHT-BODIED ————————————— FULL-BODIED

▬▬ Heller-Trum Schlenkerla Rauchbier Märzen

With their beech-smoked malts, Heller-Trum's beers have a powerful, penetrating smokiness that some find challenging. Their märzen is a copper-colored, medium-bodied lager, with a delicious dry smokiness running through it.
Country: Germany
ABV: 5.1%; Serving temp.: 48–52°

LIGHT ————————————— DARK

LIGHT-BODIED ————————————— FULL-BODIED

▬▬ Alaskan Smoked Porter

This superb seasonal beer seems to be getting harder to find. A shame, because the dry, phenolic smokiness working against the slightly sweet maltiness is a treat. Roasted grain, coffee, chocolate, cola, peat smoke, faintly resinous hops, and an odd but enjoyable savory, slightly meaty edge.
Country: USA
ABV: 6.5%; Serving temp.: 50–55°

LIGHT ————————————— DARK

LIGHT-BODIED ————————————— FULL-BODIED

▬▬ Spezial Rauchbier Märzen

The inattentive or (heaven forbid) intoxicated could easily miss the slight smokiness to the nose of this hazy copper-colored beer, layered as it is with graininess and a slight honeyed quality. The palate is soft, smoky, and slightly honeyed (again). Delicate and elegant, the smoke is always present but never dominates.
Country: Germany
ABV: 4.6%; Serving temp.: 48–52°

LIGHT ————————————— DARK

LIGHT-BODIED ————————————— FULL-BODIED

➕ Meantime Wintertime Winter Welcome

Although the label suggests drinking this after a trip out on a cold day, that's not strictly necessary. Fruits, smoke, and a little cola on the nose lead to a medium-bodied palate with coffee and chocolate flavors and a fruity-smoky finish.
Country: England
ABV: 5.4%; Serving temp.: 50–55°

LIGHT ————————————— DARK

LIGHT-BODIED ————————————— FULL-BODIED

spiced beer

The first three beers in this spread all display pronounced spice character, not cunningly created by clever hop additions but by simply adding spices to the brew. It's an ancient practice that has fallen out of fashion. Although we still mull wine during the winter months, no one thinks to mull beer—Morocco Ale would be a good starting point. Innis & Gunn is listed here partly by default, but also because it has a sweet vanilla oak spice character. Old Crafty Hen is also a beer that has seen some wood and carries the tart dryness well.

Juniper berries are an unconventional flavoring, but they can add a Scandinavian twist to a beer

🇳🇴 Haandbryggeriet Norwegian Wood

Sometimes, you read a description of a beer and think "that'll never work in a million years." Smoked malt and juniper berries are the odd couple here, but to spectacular effect. Copper-brown and very full-bodied; slightly astringent mid-palate; and a dry, peppery, and warming finish.

Food match: go Scandinavian— smoked venison, pickled herring, or gravlax
Country: Norway
ABV: 6%; Serving temp.: 50-53°

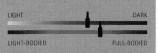

LIGHT / DARK
LIGHT-BODIED / FULL-BODIED

✚ Daleside Morocco Ale

Dating back to the mid-1800s, this ruddy-dark ale used to be matured for 21 years, then downed in one gulp as a pledge to the House of Levens. Happily, things change. Brewed with ginger and other spices, it has a dry, spicy palate with a faintly floral, perfumed edge.
Country: England
ABV: 5.5%; Serving temp.: 55°

LIGHT / DARK
LIGHT-BODIED / FULL-BODIED

🏴󠁧󠁢󠁳󠁣󠁴󠁿 Innis & Gunn Oak Aged Beer

This golden-orange beer divides drinkers. The haters complain about the lack of beer flavors and the sweetness. The lovers like the unique mix of citrus, oak, honey, vanilla, and coconut aromas and flavors. New batches seem drier of late, so perhaps it will collect more lovers than haters.
Country: Scotland
ABV: 6.6%; Serving temp.: 45-50°

LIGHT / DARK
LIGHT-BODIED / FULL-BODIED

✚ Nethergate Augustinian Ale

An unusual English abbey-style ale, slightly hazy and amber-orange in color. Soft nutty malt nose, with some zesty hop spice. Rich, slightly sweet and a little unctuous on the tongue, with quite a lot of spice (coriander) showing through. Long finish, with lots of coriander seed flavor.
Country: England
ABV: 5.2%; Serving temp.: 50-55°

LIGHT / DARK
LIGHT-BODIED / FULL-BODIED

✚ Greene King Morland Old Crafty Hen

A blend of Old Speckled Hen and Old 5X, a constituent beer in Greene King Strong Suffolk Vintage Ale (see separate entry). The classic malty Greene King aroma (pear drops) leads to a palate that is rounded, robust, and raisiny, with some oaky dryness in the finish.
Country: England
ABV: 6.5%; Serving temp.: 50-55°

LIGHT / DARK
LIGHT-BODIED / FULL-BODIED

scottish esoterica

OK, this is an unusual collection of beers, but somehow listing the classic wee heavy Skull Splitter alongside other Scottish ales seemed to do it down a little—it should really be put on a plinth and venerated as a classic of the style. The three beers from Williams Bros. are, along with the spiced beers in the previous spread, an anachronism that we can all enjoy—the ingredients sound odd, but the end result is very enjoyable. Genesee Cream Ale is loosely linked to the "California Common" style in the next spread.

Kelp collected from tidepools is an unconventional innovation by Williams Bros.

🏴󠁧󠁢󠁳󠁣󠁴󠁿 Orkney Skull Splitter

There's plenty of malty fruit on the nose of this classic "wee heavy"—golden raisins, cherries, and dates, along with some winter spice. The beer is sweet and silky in the mouth, with a lovely balanced fruitiness and a long, persistently fruity finish. Great with mature hard cheeses.

Food match: the brewery boss suggests pâté, red meat dishes, and strong cheeses
Country: Scotland
ABV: 8.5%; Serving temp.: 55–60°

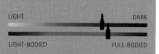

🏴󠁧󠁢󠁳󠁣󠁴󠁿 Williams Bros. Kelpie

The use of seaweed as a fertilizer in coastal communities is well known. Historically, barley grown in fields so treated developed a unique flavor. In an attempt to recreate this, Williams Bros. has added seaweed to the brew kettle. The result is a rich, dark ale with full, earthy flavor.
Country: Scotland
ABV: 5%; Serving temp.: 45–50°

🏴󠁧󠁢󠁳󠁣󠁴󠁿 Williams Bros. Alba

If some American hops give a pine-resin note to a beer, then why not the other way around? Surprisingly, it works very well, as demonstrated by this unhopped ale that derives its soft, resinous bitterness from spruce and Scotch pine (*Pinus alba*) sprigs, most notably in the finish. Unique and delicious.
Country: Scotland
ABV: 7.5%; Serving temp.: 55°

🏴󠁧󠁢󠁳󠁣󠁴󠁿 Williams Bros. Fraoch

"Brewed in Scotland since 2000 B.C." claims the label. Fortunately, brewing hygiene has moved on in the intervening two millennia. "Fraoch" (Gaelic for heather) is infused with heather flowers and the plant sweet gale. The beer has a soft perfumed top note and a dry, gently bitter finish.
Country: Scotland
ABV: 5%; Serving temp.: 55°

🇺🇸 Genesee Cream Ale

This is a nostalgic beer for me; I used to drink dollar drafts of it in New York in the early 1990s. Unsurprisingly, it no longer tastes of freedom and good times. Softly toffeeish aroma, slightly sweet and lemony palate, faintly nutty finish. Ah, my youth, where have you gone?
Country: USA
ABV: 5.1%; Serving temp.: 40–45°

oddities, rarities & specialties   273

american esoterica

Anchor Steam is an unsung icon of the American craft brewing scene. This brewery, under the stewardship of owner Fritz Maytag, started the craft brewing revolution as far back as the late 1960s. The style of beer, California Common, is the result of fermentation with a lager yeast at warm temperatures, producing soft, rounded beers. Of course, things have moved on a little in the intervening 50 years. At the other extreme, the intense, resinous character of "wet hop" ale, brewed with undried hops fresh from the harvest, have come to characterize the current American craft brewing scene.

Facilities at the Anchor Brewery in San Francisco. Steam beer, developed in the West during the Gold Rush and once produced by dozens of San Francisco breweries, is the only beer style native to the US.

🇺🇸 Anchor Brewing Steam Beer

Steam Beer is something of a hybrid, fermented with lager yeast at a warmer temperature more usual in ale brewing. The resulting copper-orange beer has a lovely orange hop character, with some toffee and butterscotch mid-palate and a sweetish marmalade finish. A classic, in a modest way.

Food match: go for an American classic—ham on rye with mustard
Country: USA
ABV: 4.8%; Serving temp.: 48–53°

🇺🇸 Flying Dog Old Scratch Amber Lager

More of an American hybrid than a thoroughbred lager, this coppery beer has an aroma of floral hops, caramel, and butterscotch (a sign of warmer fermentation temperature). Floral hops and marmalade-on-toast come through in the finish. An accessible California example.
Country: USA
ABV: 5.3%; Serving temp.: 48–53°

🇺🇸 Sierra Nevada Harvest Ale

This is brewed with undried hops, which impart an earthy, resinous quality to an already near-perfect pale ale. The result is the kind of rounded, bittersweet symphony that beer-lovers dream of, jam-packed with pithy hop goodness. Well worth seeking out.
Country: USA
ABV: 6.7%; Serving temp.: 48–53°

🇺🇸 Port Brewing High Tide

Delicious resinous hop aromas leap from the glass and goose your olfactory bulb with pine needles, sweet orange, grapefruit, and a heady floral quality. Fairly big but balanced, a powerful, pithy bitterness builds into the finish, leaving grapefruit, tangerine, and pine resin flavors.
Country: USA
ABV: 6.5%; Serving temp.: 48–53°

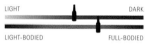

✚ Thornbridge Halcyon

Pours slightly hazy, peach-colored, with a big, persistent head. Intensely fruity aroma—orange pith, tangerine, and ripe cantaloupe, and peppery hop notes. Palate is medium-sweet, with the fruitiness carrying into the finish, which reveals more melon, pepper, and orange notes. Intense, but brilliantly fresh.
Country: England
ABV: 7.7%; Serving temp.: 50–55°

strong golden beer

This is a slightly odd group of beers, but the stronger three exemplify it best. Deus, in its champagne-style bottle and branded flute glasses, has come to be a bit of a hit in the smart restaurant set—if you're going to have a beer list, then you'd better find some fancy beer to put on it. The two weaker beers here (and I use the word weaker very much in a relative sense) are favorites of mine— they're not the rarest or strongest beers in the world, but they do have plenty of character, and you don't have to pay the earth for them.

Beekeeping has been practiced for almost 5000 years. Today honey is sometimes added to beer early in the brewing process; it adds a light, perfumed edge, not necessarily a strong sweetness.

▓▓ Bosteels Deus Brut Des Flandres

Deus is a lively golden beer, with a pronounced pale stone fruit character (peaches and apricots) and an exceptional intensity. Matured before release in subterranean caves and designed to be served ice-cold in champagne flutes, it's a very convincing stab at a luxury cuvée.

Food match: canapes—goat cheese crostini, black olives, anchovy toast
Country: Belgium
ABV: 11.5%; Serving temp.: 38–42°

LIGHT | DARK
LIGHT-BODIED | FULL-BODIED

▓▓ Grain D'orge Belzebuth

This beer (at 13%abv) should really be a raucous, sticky mess, but far from it. There is a peppery whiff of alcohol on the nose and an almost mentholated chest-clearing quality to the palate. Surprisingly, the finish is fairly dry, with some bitterness and an unsurprising warmth.
Country: France
ABV: 13%; Serving temp.: 48–53°

LIGHT | DARK
LIGHT-BODIED | FULL-BODIED

▓▓ Lefebvre Barbar

Barbar is a lovely example of a honey beer. The use of honey as a source of fermentable sugar is a traditional technique, and the floral qualities of the honey are easy to find on the nose of this pale golden beer. On the palate, there is a little residual sweetness, but this is not at all cloying. The floral note returns in the finish.
Country: Belgium
ABV: 8%; Serving temp.: 48–53°

LIGHT | DARK
LIGHT-BODIED | FULL-BODIED

▓▓ Gayant La Biere Du Demon

The label declares "12 Degrees of Devilish Pleasure." You can tell it's a strong beer from the heady pale malt and alcohol aroma; the sweet, slightly sticky palate; and the warming effect in the finish (which has an almost schnapps-like numbing sensation).
Country: France
ABV: 12%; Serving temp.: 48–53°

LIGHT | DARK
LIGHT-BODIED | FULL-BODIED

▓▓ St Sylvestre 3 Monts

This is a nice, gutsy example of the style. Pouring golden, there is a sense of both power and balance to the aroma – lots of malt, hop, and a little alcohol. The palate has some sweetness but a good hop bite, which combines with the alcohol to give a spicy, peppery finish.
Country: France
ABV: 8.5%; Serving temp.: 48–53°

LIGHT | DARK
LIGHT-BODIED | FULL-BODIED

very strong beer

The title says it all, really, if a tad prosaically. The beers in this spread are some of the strongest in this book (and indeed, the world). They are strong not only in alcohol, but their flavors are intense too. There are stronger beers than the barrel-aged Pannepot Grand Reserva, but it delivers such a burst of intense fruity flavor that it challenges the notion of what beer is meant to taste like. In fact, all of these beers do exactly that—they push at the boundaries of what beer can be.

Antique beer barrels on a hay cart in front of a traditional brewery

☰ Samuel Adams Utopias

Dark amber, with no carbonation, there is a huge aroma of sherry and bourbon (Utopias is multi-cask finished), oranges, caramel, wood, and maple syrup. Intensely sweet at first, with some spirit heat and a riot of barley wine, sherry, and bourbon. An icon, sure, but is it really beer?

Food match: liqueur chocolates, and a lie-down in a dark room
Country: USA
ABV: 27%; Serving temp.: 55–60°

LIGHT		DARK
LIGHT-BODIED		FULL-BODIED

☰ Mikkeller Black

Mention extreme beer, and someone will ask, "Where will it all end?" Here is as good a place as any. Pitch-black, unctuous, bursting with roasted coffee, dried fruits, and some sweet sherry aromas. Intense chocolate espresso with some hops and a warming alcohol hit. Enjoyably eccentric.
Country: Denmark
ABV: 17.5%; Serving temp.: 50–55°

LIGHT		DARK
LIGHT-BODIED		FULL-BODIED

☰ Schneider Aventinus Weizen-Eisbock

Created by freezing and removing the water in a batch of Aventinus, this is the *ne plus ultra* of wheat beer. A turbid, murky beer, bursting with aromas of caramel, toffee, butterscotch, and overripe banana. An explosion of flavor leaves cinnamon, figs, brandy, black pepper, and marzipan.
Country: Germany
ABV: 12%; Serving temp.: 49–54°

LIGHT		DARK
LIGHT-BODIED		FULL-BODIED

☰ Schloss Eggenberg Samichlaus

Brewed every December 6 and matured for a year prior to release. A copper-tawny color, the huge heady aroma of golden raisins and sherry wafts out of the glass. Best served in a balloon glass, this is massive, sweet, and warming. Perfect with a slab of Christmas cake.
Country: Austria
ABV: 14%; Serving temp.: 55–60°

LIGHT		DARK
LIGHT-BODIED		FULL-BODIED

☰ Struise Pannepot Grand Reserva 2005

There is a lot of hype around this barrel-aged version of Pannepot, and deservedly so. Figs, prunes, and black cherries fill the aroma, while the palate is a burst of these fruits, with some winter spices to boot. The finish dries a little but is intense, vinous, and persistent. Incredible.
Country: Belgium
ABV: 10%; Serving temp.: 50–55°

LIGHT		DARK
LIGHT-BODIED		FULL-BODIED

oddities, rarities & specialties   279

index

A

Abbaye Des Rocs Blanche Des Honnelles 143
abbey & Trappist dubbel 208-13
abbey & Trappist tripel 200-6
abbey beers 167, 197-219, 211, 212
abbey blonde beer 198-9
AB-Inbev 141
AB-Inbev Staropramen 63
AB-Inbev Stella Artois 76
Achel brewery 197
Achelse Kluis Achel Blonde 206
Achelse Kluis Achel Brune 213
Achouffe La Chouffe 168, 169
Acorn Barnsley Bitter 108
Adams, Samuel 90
adjunct 12
Adnams 226
Adnams Broadside 227
Alaskan Smoked Porter 269
ale 12
Alhambra 1925 Reserve 72
Alhambra Negra 94
altbier 34, 260, 262
Alvinne Podge, Belgian Beer Tours 245
Alvinne Podge Belgian Imperial Stout 245
Alvinne Tripel 205
American esoterica 274-5
American pale ale 180-1
Anchor Brewery, San Francisco 274
Anchor Brewing 234
Anchor Brewing Liberty Ale 132
Anchor Brewing Old Foghorn 226, 227
Anchor Brewing Porter 239
Anchor Brewing Steam Beer 275
Anchor Old Foghorn 45
Anchor Steam 32-4, 274

Anchor Tavern, London 244
Andechs Brewery 264
Andechs Doppelbock Dunkel 98
Andechs Spezial Hell 84, 85
Arioli, Agostino 164
aroma 54
aroma hops 12, 39
Asahi Black 94
Asahi building, Tokyo 95
Asahi Dry 79
Asia Pacific Tiger 80, 81
Asia Pacific Tui East India Pale Ale 184
Atlas Latitude Highland Pilsner 129
Atlas Three Sisters 139
attack 12
Ayinger Celebrator Doppelbock 98
Ayinger Weizen Bock 151

B

Babylonia 6
Badger Tanglefoot 130
Ballast Point Black Marlin Porter 239
Ballast Point Brewery 238
barley 12, 21, 23, 24-7
roasting 208, 234
barley wine 221, 222-5, 226
barrel-aged beer see cask-aged beer
barrel-aging 12
barrel flora 12, 153, 265
barrels 73, 80, 264, 278
Bateman Salem Porter 236
Batemans XXXB 107
Bateman Victory Ale 114
Bavik Petrus Oud Bruin 155
beekeeping 276
beer gardens, Germany 148
beer stein 77
Belgian ales 170-1
strong 172-3, 266

Belgium 34, 57, 142, 153, 158, 167-77, 170
Belhaven Twisted Thistle 188
Bells Two Hearted Ale 191
Bernard Kvasnicove Svetly Lezak 83
Birrificio Italiano 164
Birrificio Italiano Amber Shock 97
Birrificio Italiano Bibock 97
Birrificio Italiano Cassissona 165
Birrificio Italiano Scires 165
Birrificio Italiano Tipopils 68, 69
bitter 102-9
bittering hops 13, 37
Black Diamond Amber Ale 104
Black Sheep Bitter Ale 108
Black Sheep Riggwelter 132
Black Sheep Yorkshire Square Ale 135
Blueford Bitter 103
bock and doppelbock 84, 90, 96-8
body 13
Bohemia Regent President 87
Bohemia Regent Tmavy 93
Bolten Alt 262
Bolten Ur-Alt 262
Bolten Ur-Weizen 145
Boon Gueuze 160
Bosteels Deus Brut Des Flandres 276, 277
Bosteels Kwak 172, 173
Bosteels Tripel Karmeliet 202
bottle caps 172
bottle-conditioned beer 49
bottle-conditioning 13
Box Steam Brewery Dark & Handsome 227
Brains Dark 114
Brains SA Gold 119
Brakspear Bitter 107
Brakspear brewery 230
Brakspear Triple 231

Brasserie Dupont Avec Les Bons Voeux 169
Brasserie Dupont Saison Dupont 169
Brauerei Hirt Hirter Privat Pils 64
Brettanomyces bruxellensis 13, 15, 32, 34
BrewDog Paradox Imperial Stout 246
BrewDog Punk IPA 188
BrewDog Rip Tide Stout 249
BrewDog Trashy Blonde 126
BrewDog Zeitgeist 94
breweries 41
Chinese 80
tours and visits 40
brewing kettle 13, 38
brewing process 6, 27, 37-9
quality control 118
brewing vessels, Bohemian brewery 92
Bridge of Allan Glencoe Wild Oat Stout 257
Bridge of Allan Tullibardine 1488 Whisky Ale 265
British beer 101-39
Brooklyn Black Chocolate Stout 246
Brooklyn Brown Ale 111
Brooklyn Lager 89
Brooklyn Local 1 175
brown ale 57, 110-11
Bruges
Café Vlissinghe 175
De Gouden Boon 177
town hall 154
Brussels 153, 158, 266
Grand' Place 198
Budweiser Budvar 64
Budweiser Budvar Dark 94
Burton, water 22
Burton Bridge Brewery Bramble Stout 252
Burton Bridge Brewery Empire Pale Ale 187

Burton Bridge Brewery Porter 236
buying beer 46

C

Cail, Stuart 125
Cairngorm Trade Winds 119
Caledonian Deuchars IPA 129
California Common 32, 274
CAMRA (Campaign for Real Ale) 13, 49, 128, 131
Cantillon brewery, logo 162
Cantillon Gueuze 158, 160
Caracole Nostradamus 169
Caracole Saxo 175
carbonation 13, 53
Carlsberg Carnegie Stark Porter 236
Carlton & United Victoria Bitter 76
Cascade 31
cask-aged beer 259, 264–5
cask-aging 14
cask ale 14
caviar 248
Celis, Pierre 141
Celis White 141
Cerveceria Mexicana Red Pig Mexican Ale 184
Chang Export 81
Chimay Blue 217
Chimay brewery 197
Chimay Red 215
Chimay White 206
Chinook 31
chocolate malt 247
Christmas beer 259, 266–7
Christoffel Blonde 68, 69
Christoffel Robertus 89
civet 14
cloudiness 141
Clyde, river, Glasgow, brewery 124
coffee beans 14, 254
Cologne 260
color of beer 46, 53, 55, 197
condition 14
Coney Island, Brooklyn, New York 88

Coniston Bluebird 103
Coniston Bluebird XB 103
Cooper's Best Extra Stout 251
Cooper's Dark 231
Cooper's Pale Ale 123
Cooper's Sparkling Ale 123
Cooper's Vintage Ale 136
Coors Kasteel Cru 82, 83
Copper Dragon Golden Pippin 129
copper mash tun 70
Coreff Ambrée 131
Cornell, Martyn 179
Cornish Gold malt 132
craft brewing 14
Cropton Balmy Mild 117
Cropton Blackout Porter 235
Crouch Vale Brewer's Gold 126
Czech Republic 22

D

Daleside Blonde 125
Daleside Morocco Ale 270, 271
Daleside Ripon Jewel 132
Dark Star Espresso Stout 255
Dark Star Hophead 126
Dark Star Saison 169
De Dolle Brouwers Arabier 176
De Dolle Brouwers Extra Stout 249
De Dolle Brouwers Stille Nacht 267
De Halve Maan Brugse Zot 199
De Halve Maan Brugse Zot Dubbel 209
De Koninck De Koninck 170, 171
Delhi, Red Fort 185
De Molen Tsarina Esra Imperial Porter 240, 241
Dent T'owd Tup 228
De Ranke XX Bitter 170, 171
Deschutes Black Butte Porter 236
Deschutes The Dissident 155
Deschutes Inversion IPA 192
Deschutes Mirror Pond Pale Ale 181
Deschutes Obsidian 252

Deschutes Twilight Ale 184
Desnoes & Geddes Dragon Stout 256, 257
De Struise & Mikkeller Elliot Brew 206
Dinkelacker-Schwaben Märzen 87
Dinkelacker-Schwaben Meister Pils 63
Dinkelacker-Schwaben Privat 85
Dinkelacker-Schwaben Das Schwarze 93
Dogfish Head 60 Minute IPA 191
Dogfish Head Indian Brown Ale 111
Dom Kölsch 261
doppelbock 84, 90, 98
draft ale 130
Dreher, Anton 88
drinkability 14
Du Bocq Corsendonk Agnus-Tripel 201
Du Bocq Corsendonk Christmas 267
Du Bocq Corsendonk Pater-Dubbel 209
Dubuisson Bush 173
Duchy Originals Organic Ale 135
Duchy Originals Winter Ale 135
Durham Cloister 119
Durham Evensong 131
Düsseldorf 260

E

East Kent Golding 31
Egypt 6
Einbeck, Germany 96, 96
Elland Beyond the Pale 125
Ellezelloise Hercule Stout 249
Ellezelloise Saisis 143
Ename Blonde 199
Ename Dubbel 209
Erdinger Pikantus 151
Erdinger Schneeweisse 145
Erdinger Weissbier 146
Erdinger Weissbier Dunkel 149

ester 14
Exmoor Ales Exmoor Gold 118, 119
extra special bitter (ESB) 112–15
extreme beer 15

F

farmhouse ale 168–9
faro 153
Faversham, Kent, hop festival, morris dancers 121
Feierling Brewery, Freiburg, Germany 38
Felinfoel Double Dragon 108
fermentable sugar 135
fermentation 15, 32, 39, 61, 135
cold 34
spontaneous 19
finish 15
Firestone Walker 181
First Gold hops 103
Flanders 153
flavor 54
Flemish brown ale 154–6
Flying Dog Brewery 225
Flying Dog Doggie Style Classic Pale Ale 181
Flying Dog Gonzo Imperial Porter 240, 241
Flying Dog Horn Dog 224
Flying Dog Old Scratch Amber Lager 275
Flying Dog Snake Dog IPA 192
foam content 52
food, beer and 45, 57–58
Franconia 27, 263
Frankenheim Alt 262
Frederick, Maryland 225
Freedom Organic Dark Lager 89
Freising Huber Weisses Original 149
Freistädter Brewery, Austria 26
fruit beers, non-lambic 164–5
Fuggles 31
Fuller's Brewer's Reserve No. 1 265
Fuller's ESB 112, 113

Fuller's Gale's Prize Old Ale 228
Fuller's Vintage Ale 223
funk, funky 15
Furstenberg Export 67

G
Gaffel Kölsch 261
Gayant La Biere du Demon 277
Genesee Cream Ale 273
German regional specialties 260–3
Germany 27, 144
germinating 16
Gilbert, John 120
Girardian Faro 1882 163
Girardin Gueuze Black Label 1882 160
glass
    angling 142
    shape of 50, 53, 167
golden ale, strong 174–6, 276–7
Golden Promise barley 24
Goose Island 214
Goose Island Bourbon County Brand Stout 244, 245
Goose Island Honkers Ale 104
Goose Island IPA 187
Goose Island Matilda 215
Gordon Biersch Blonde Bock 97
Gordon Biersch Hefeweizen 149
Gordon Biersch Märzen 87
Gordon Biersch Pilsner 69
Gormley, Antony 104
    Angel of the North 105
Gosser Export 71
Grain D'orge Belzebuth 277
Grand Teton Bitch Creek ESB 114
Great American Beer Festival (GABF) 15
Great British Beer Festival (GBBF) 15, 116, 129
Great Divide Titan IPA 195
Great Divide Yeti Imperial Stout 246
Greene King Morland Old Crafty Hen 270, 271

Greene King Strong Suffolk Vintage Ale 228
Greene King XX Mild 117
Grimbergen Blonde 199
Grimbergen Cuvée De L'Ermitage 170, 171
Grimbergen Optimo Bruno 219
grist 16, 17
Grolsch Grolsch Premium 76
Grolsch Weizen 146
gueuze 153
Guinness 57, 233
    Brewery 256
    Draught 257
Guinness Special Export 251

H
Haandbryggeriet IPA 183
Haandbryggeriet Norwegian Wood 271
Haandbryggeriet Porter 241
Hacker-Pschorr Hefe-Weisse 149
Hacker-Pschorr Munchner Gold 76
Hacker-Pschorr Oktoberfest Märzen 87
Hacker-Pschorr Superior Festbier 85
Hahn Premium 71
Hall & Woodhouse Badger First Gold 103
Hall & Woodhouse Badger Tanglefoot 132
Hallertau Valley, Germany 29, 31, 61
Hambleton Nightmare Stout 251
hangover 16
Hanssens Oude Kriek 159
Harpoon Brewery, Boston 189
Harpoon IPA 188
Hartwall Lapin Kulta 79
Harvey's Sussex Best 103
Harviestoun Bitter & Twisted 125
Harviestoun Ola Dubh 12yr Old 265

Harviestoun Ola Dubh 30yr Old 265
haze, hazy 16
heather 273
Heineken Export 71
Heineken Krusovice Imperial 64
Heineken Zagorka Special 75
Heller-Trum brewery 259, 268
Heller-Trum Schlenkerla Rauchbier Märzen 269
Heller-Trum Schlenkerla Rauchbier Urbock 259, 269
helles and helles-bock 84–5
Hersbrucker hop 71
Het Anker Gouden Carolus Classic 173
Het Anker Gouden Carolus Tripel 206
High Falls JW Dundee Honey Brown 91
Highland Brewing Orkney Blast 188
Highland Brewing Orkney Porter 241
Hoegaarden Brewery 141, 142
Hoegaarden Forbidden Fruit 173
Hoegaarden Grand Cru 176
Hoegaarden Wit 143
Hogs Back A over T 223
Hogs Back Traditional English Ale (TEA) 108
Holden's Black Country Mild 114
honey 276, 277
Hook Norton Double Stout 252
Hook Norton Old Hooky 107
hop back 16
Hop Back Entire Stout 252
Hop Back Summer Lightning 118, 120
hop gardens 127
hop-growing 180, 263
hops 16, 21, 23, 28–31, 37–9, 74, 179
    bittering 13, 37
    dried 182
    wet 274
Horseshoe Falls, Tasmania 78

Huyghe Delirium Noel 267
Huyghe Delirium Tremens 175

I
"Ichiban Shibori" brewing method 79
't IJ Columbus 215
't IJ Natte 210
't IJ Scharrel IJwit 143
't IJ Zatte 201
Ilkley Moor, Yorkshire 109
India Pale Ale (IPA) 57, 179–92
    double/imperial 194–5
ingredients 13–35, 37
Innis & Gunn Oak Aged Beer 270, 271
Isle of Skye Black Cuillin 139
Isle of Skye Hebridean Bold 123

J
Jackson, Michael 15
James Boag's Premium 79
Jever Dark 93
Jever Pilsner 45, 63
John Martin Gordon Xmas 267
juniper berries 270
JW Lees Harvest Ale 224
JW Lees Moonraker 223

K
Kaltenberg König Ludwig Dunkel 93
keg beer 16, 128
Kelham Island Brooklyn Smoked Porter 243
kelp 272
Keo Keo 83
kilning 17
Kirin Ichiban 79
kölsch 34, 260, 261–2
Kootenai River Valley, Idaho 180
Kopi Luwak coffee beans 14
Köstritzer Schwarzbier 93
Krakus Zywiec 75
kriek 57

Krönleins Crocodile 72
Kross Pilsner 72
Kulmbacher Monchshof
  Landbier 67
Küppers Kölsch 261

L

lager 17, 32, 34, 61–99, 101
  Asian 80–1
  black 61, 90, 92–5
  dark 90
  golden 61, 62
  oddments 90–1
  pilsner-style 70–9
  temperature 51
  Vienna-style 27, 88–9, 90
  yeasts 32
lager yeast 32
lambic beer 34, 83, 153,
  158–63, 161, 221, 233
Lao Brewery Beer Lao 81
late yeast 32
lautering 17, 37
Lebkuchen hearts 86
Le Coq, Albert 244
Leeds Midnight Bell 117
Lefebvre Barbar 277
Leffe Blonde 198, 199
Leffe Brewery 203
Leffe Brune 210
Leffe Radieuse 210
Leffe Triple 202
Leuven, Belgium 203
Liefmans Frambozen 156
Liefmans Goudenband 155
Liefmans Kriek 45, 156
Lindeboom Pilsener 71
Lindemans brewery, Belgium
  157
Lindemans Gueuze Cuvée
  René 163
Lindemans Pecheresse 154, 156
Lion Lion Stout 249
liquor 17
Little Creatures Pale Ale 184
London, water 22
Luitpold, Prince of Bavaria 93

M

McEwans Champion 139
macro 17
Madonna 108
Magic Hat #9 165
Mahou Cinco Estrellas 79
Maibock 136
Maisel's Dunkel 149
Maisel's Weisse 146
malt 17, 21, 24–7, 61, 101, 179
  sacks 110
maltster 17
Malzmühle Kölsch 262
Maris Otter barley 24
Marston's Owd Rodger 231
Marston's Pedigree 107
märzen/Oktoberfest 86–7, 88
mash 17, 37
mash tun 18
Maytag, Fritz 274
Meantime IPA 187
Meantime London Porter 235
Meantime Wintertime
  Welcome 269
meats, salted and cured 268
Meux Brewery, London 233
Mikkeller 214
Mikkeller All Others Pale 192
Mikkeller Beer Geek Breakfast
  Pooh Coffee Cask Festival
  Edition 255
Mikkeller Beer Geek Breakfast
  "Weasel" 255
Mikkeller Black 279
Mikkeller It's Alive! 215
mild 116–17
Modelo Negra Modelo 89
Monteith's New Zealand
  Lager 75
Moorhouse's Black Cat 45, 117
Moorhouse's English Owd
  Ale 231
Moorhouse's Pendle Witches
  Brew 120
Moortgat Duvel 45, 174,
  175, 199
Moortgat Maredsous 6 199
Moortgat Maredsous 8 210
Moortgat Maredsous 10 205
Moritz Moritz 72

mouthfeel 18
Mt. Shasta Mountain High
  IPA 191
Munich 88
  Oktoberfest 86, 86, 137
mushroom risotto 250
Mythos Mythos 71

N

Naylor's Pinnacle Porter 235
Nelson Sauvin hop 123
Nethergate Augustinian
  Ale 271
Nethergate Old Growler 236
New Glarus Raspberry Tart 156
New Glarus Wisconsin Belgian
  Red 156
New Zealand 74
Nils Oscar Barley Wine 223
Nils Oscar Imperial Stout 245
Nils Oscar Rökporter 243
nitrogenation 18
Nøgne Ø Imperial Stout 249
Nøgne Ø Porter 234, 239
Nørrebro brewery, Copenhagen
  186
Nørrebro Bryghus Bombay Pale
  Ale 187

O

Oakham JHB 126
oast houses 30–1
Obatzda 144
Obolon Deep Velvet 94
oddities, rarities & specialties
  259–79
O'Hanlons Port Stout 255
O'Hanlons Thomas Hardy's Ale
  45, 224
Okells Smoked Porter 243
Oktoberfestbier 86–7, 88
old ale 221, 226–31, 233
Orkney Dark Island 139
Orkney Dark Island Reserve 265
Orkney Islands 138
Orkney Skullsplitter 138,
  272, 273
Orval, abbey 214

Orval brewery 197
Orval Orval 215
Ossett Treacle Stout 255
Otley O-Ho-Ho 120
Oude Beersel Gueuze Vieille
  160
Outlaw Dead or Alive IPA 183
Outlaw Wild Mule 125
oysters 242

P

palate 18
pale ale, American 180–1
pale golden ale 118–23
Palm 170, 177
Palm Brugge Triple 176
Palm Royale 176
Palm Speciale 171
Panimoravintola Huvila ESB
  114, 115
Panimoravintola Huvila Porter
  239
pasteurization 18
Pattinson, Ron 179
Paulaner Hefe-Weissbier 146
Paulaner Original Munchner
  Hell 85
Paulaner Salvator 98
Pelforth Brune 210
Pennsylvania, USA 68
peppermint stout 254
percentage abv 12
Peroni Gran Riserva 97
Peroni Nastro Azzurro 76
Pietra Pietra 72
Pike, The (Brakspear's pub) 230
Pilsen brewery, central Europe
  65
pilsner 22, 45, 61, 62–7, 66, 101
  "new wave" 68–9
Pilsner Urquell Brewery, Czech
  Republic 62
pitching 18
pith 18
PJ Früh Kölsch 261
Plzensky Prazdroj Pilsner
  Urquell 64
Point Loma, California 238
Pollard, Chris 245

Port Brewing 240
Port Brewing High Tide 275
Port Brewing Hop 15 195
Port Brewing Old Viscosity
  240, 241
porter 233, 234–9, 237
  imperial 240–1
  smoked 242–3, 242
pubs, traditional 132
Purple Moose Snowdonia
  Ale 129

R

Rauchbier *see* smoked beer
real ale 18, 49
Reinheitsgebot 19
rice 80
Ridgeway Foreign Export
  Stout 251
Riva Vondel 155
Robinson's Double Hop 113
Robinson's Old Tom 231
Rochefort brewery 197, 216
Rochefort Rochefort 6 217
Rochefort Rochefort 8 217
Rochefort Rochefort 8 217
Rochefort Rochefort 10 217
Rodenbach 158
Rodenbach Grand Cru 159
Rodenbach Rodenbach 159
Rogue Brutal Bitter 113
Rogue Dead Guy Ale 136
Rogue Morimoto Black Obi
  Soba Ale 131
Roosters YPA 126
Rothaus Märzen 87
Rothaus Pils 67
Rothbauer, Volker, "Brew
  Owl" 150
Rudgate Ruby Mild 117
Russia 244
Russian River 158
Russian River Beatification 160
Russian River Supplication
  (Batch 003) 159
rye 194

S

Saaz 31, 61, 64, 69
Saccharomyces cerevisae 32
Saccharomyces uvarum 32
St Austell Admiral's Ale 132
St Austell Proper Job 183
St Austell Tribute 125
St. Bernardus 208
St. Bernardus Abt 12 219
St. Bernardus Pater 6 213
St. Bernardus Prior 8 213
St. Bernardus Tripel 209
St Peter's Cream Stout 252
St Sylvestre 3 Monts 277
saisons 168–9, 168
Saku Porter 234, 235
Saltaire Cascade 188
Saltaire Hazelnut Coffee Porter
  242, 243
Samuel Adams Boston Lager
  90, 91
Samuel Adams Utopia 279
Samuel Smith's Imperial Stout
  45, 244, 245
Samuel Smith's Nut Brown
  Ale 111
Samuel Smith's Oatmeal
  Stout 257
Samuel Smith's Pure Brewed
  Lager 69
Samuel Smith's Taddy Porter
  243
Samuel Smith's Yorkshire
  Stingo 136
Sapporo Premium 75
Savolinna Castle, Finland 115
Schloss Eggenberg Samichlaus
  279
Schloss Eggenberg Urbock
  230 97
Schlosser Alt 262
Schneider Aventinus 151
Schneider Aventinus Weizen-
  Eisbock 279
Schneider Schneider &
  Brooklyner Hopfen-Weisse
  151
Schneider Weisse wheat beer
  45, 145

Schönram Festweisse 151
Schönram Original Altbayerisch
  Dunkel 91
Schönram Pils 63
Schremser Doppelmalz 91
Schremser Roggen Bio Bier 83
Scottish & Newcastle
  Newcastle Brown 111
Scottish ale 101, 138–9
Scottish esoterica 272–3
seaweed 273
Sedlmayr, Gabriel 88
selecting beer 45–6
serving beer 49–50
session beer 19, 124–9
Sharp's Chalky's Bite 120
Sharp's Cornish Coaster 129
Sharp's Massive Ale 224
Shepherd Neame Christmas
  Ale 267
Shepherd Neame Spitfire 103
The Ship and Shovel, Charing
  Cross station, London 106
Shmaltz Coney Island Lager 89
Shmaltz He'brew Bittersweet
  Lenny's RIPA 195
Shmaltz He'brew Genesis
  Ale 181
Shmaltz He'brew Messiah
  Bold 111
Shongweni Robson's Durban
  Pale Ale 184
Sierra Nevada Bigfoot 224
Sierra Nevada Harvest Ale 275
Sierra Nevada Pale Ale 181
Sierra Nevada Porter 239
Sierra Nevada Stout 251
Singha Premium 81
Sixpoint Bengal IPA 191
Sixpoint Brownstone 112, 113
smoked beer (Rauchbier) 27,
  259, 268–9
sour red beers 158–63
Southwold, Suffolk 226
Spalt 31, 61
sparging 19, 37
speakeasy bars 193
Speakeasy Big Daddy IPA 192

Speakeasy Double Daddy
  Imperial IPA 195
Speakeasy Prohibition Ale 113
Speakeasy Untouchable Pale
  Ale 183
Spezial Rauchbier Märzen 269
spiced beer 270–1
Stammtisch 148
steak pie 253
Stein, Rick 120
Stella Artois brewery 203
Stieglbrauerei Stiegl Bier 64
Stone Imperial Russian Stout
  246
Stone IPA 191
storing beer 49
stout 43, 57, 233, 250–7
  flavored 254–5
  imperial 244–9
  oatmeal 256–7
strength of beer 46, 197
strong ales 130–6
strong golden beer 174–6,
  276–7
Strubbe Crombe Oud
  Kriekenbier 159
Struise Pannepot Grand
  Reserva 2005 278, 279
Sumeria 6
Sünner Kölsch 261
Svaneke Sejlor Øl 82, 83
Svyturys-Utenos Porteris 235

T

tasting 53–4
Taybeh Golden 75
temperature 49
Tettnang 31, 63
Tettnanger 61
Theakstons Old Peculier 227
Thornbridge Bracia 135
Thornbridge Halcyon 275
Thornbridge Jaipur 183
Thornbridge Kipling 123
Thornbridge St. Petersburg
  Imperial Russian Stout 245
Thrale's 244
Timmermans 158

Timmermans Blanche Lambicus 163
Timmermans Faro 163
Timmermans Gueuze Tradition 163
Timothy Taylor Landlord 108
La Trappe Blond 201
La Trappe brewery 197
La Trappe Dubbel 213
La Trappe Quadrupel 219
La Trappe Tripel 202
Trappist & abbey quadrupel 218–19
Trappist ale 214–15
dark 216–17
Trappist beers 167, 197–219
Traquair House Ale 228
Traquair Jacobite Ale 228
Trunk Vierzehnheiligen Silberbock Hell 85
Tsingtao Tsingtao 81

U
"un-lager" 82–3
Unibroue La Fin Du Monde 202
United States of America 179
hops 31
Urthel Hibernus Quentum Tripel 205
Urthel Hop-It 176
Urthel Samaranth Quadrupel 219

V
Val-Dieu Triple 205
Van Eecke Poperings Hommel 170, 171
Van Honsebrouck Brigand IPA 187
Van Honsebrouck Kasteel Bruin 173
Van Honsebrouck Kasteel Triple 175
Van Steenberge 135
Van Steenberge Augustijn 201
Van Steenberge Augustijn Grand Cru 209
Van Steenberge Celis Wit 143

Verhaeghe Duchesse De Bourgogne 155
very strong beer 278–9
Victory Golden Monkey 202
Victory Hop Devil IPA 45, 192
Victory Hop Wallop 195
Victory Prima Pils 69
Vienna malt 27

W
Wadworth 6X 107
Warsteiner Premium 67
water 19, 21, 22–3, 23
Weihenstephaner Hefe Weissbier 146
Weihenstephaner Hefe Weissbier Hell 145
Weihenstephaner Korbinian 98
Weihenstephaner Kristall Weissbier 145
weissbier 57, 83, 141, 144–7
weissbock 150
weizenbock 150
well-hopped "session" beers 124–9
Wells & Young's Bombardier 131
Wells & Young's Double Chocolate Stout 255
Wells & Young's Young's Kew Gold 123
Wells, Charles 135
Weltenburger Kloster Asam Bock 98
Weltenburger Kloster Hefe-Weissbier Hell 145
Weltenburger Kloster Winter-Traum 91
Wensleydale Black Dub 257
Westmalle, Belgium
brewery 197
castle 207
Westmalle Dubbel 213
Westmalle Tripel 200, 206
Westvleteren, Sint Sixtus abbey 200
Westvleteren Abt 12 219
Westvleteren Blond 201
Westvleteren brewery 197

Westvleteren Extra 8 217
wet hop ale 274
wheat beer 45, 140, 141–9, 145, 147
wild & fruity 153–65
wild yeasts 32, 34, 39
Williams Bros. 272
Williams Bros. Alba 273
Williams Bros. Ebulum 165
Williams Bros. Fraoch 273
Williams Bros. Grozet 165
Williams Bros. Kelpie 273
winter warmers 266
witbier 141, 142–3
Wolf Best Bitter 104
Wolf Golden Jackal 119
Woodforde's Head Cracker 223
Woodforde's Norfolk Nog 227
Woodforde's Sherry 104
wort 17, 19, 37–9
Worthington White Shield 136
Wychwood Hobgoblin 131
Wylam Angel 104
Wyndham Arms, Salisbury 120

Y
yeast 13, 32–5, 33, 35, 36, 39, 190
bottom-fermenting 13, 17, 61
top-fermenting 19, 101
wild 19, 153, 221
Young's brewery 122
Young's Special London Ale 135

Z
Zatecky Pivovar Zatec 63

recommended reading

Rather than provide a definitive list of beer books, I've listed below the authors whose books I've enjoyed. They not only write engagingly, but also have a great knowledge of their specialist area. It may also be worth searching the web, as many maintain blogs:

Michael Jackson—not "the gloved one", but the original Beer Hunter
Roger Protz—beer guides, world beers, and a great autobiography
Jeff Evans—beer guides, almanacs and beer-related trivia
Ben McFarland—global beer (especially the West Coast of the US)
Pete Brown—wry social and historical writing about beer
Adrian Tierney-Jones—global beer and beer guides

However, two books that I've found myself returning to time and again are:

Michael Jackson, *Beer Companion*. For me, the classic text about beer styles and the culture that surrounds them, elegantly written and shot through with dry humour.

Garrett Oliver, *The Brewmaster's Table: Discovering the Pleasures of Real Beer with Real Food*. The definitive book on beer and food matching, and pretty comprehensive just as a beer book. Written with characteristic brio by the brewmaster of the Brooklyn Brewery. Garrett Oliver is also editor-in-chief of what promises to be the definitive beer reference book, *The Oxford Companion to Beer*, scheduled for release in 2011.

web resources
www.ratebeer.com – avid community of beer raters, with a lot of other related information
www.beer-pages.com – Roger Protz's online home

acknowledgments

There are many people to whom I owe a huge amount of thanks, and without whom this book wouldn't be half as interesting as it is. Phil Lowry and www.beermerchants.com were both helpful and generous in helping to source rarer beers. The good people at Utobeer in London's Borough Market were also a great help, as were the kind folk at Beer Paradise and www.beerritz.co.uk. No beer book is complete without thanking the redoubtable Jeff Pickthall, so thanks Jeff. Andreas Fält at Vertical Drinks, the team at James Clay, Thornbridge Brewery, Birrificio Italiano, Bob Pease at the American Brewers Association, Alex Rist for the German phone calls, and a whole host of generous people who were only to happy to drop everything and try to help with my requests, and who I've forgotten to mention by name—thank you all.

This book wouldn't have been written at all without the help of my work colleagues Dan Payne and Will Briggs, who helped run the shop in Leeds while I sat in the office, tasting beer and writing notes—I hope you both enjoyed sharing the beers, and I promise you that it was harder work than it looked.

I also owe thanks to many people for inspiration and encouragement over the years, but particular thanks go to: the late Michael "Beer Hunter" Jackson, Roger Protz, Jeff Evans, Garrett Oliver, Adrian Tierney-Jones, Rupert Ponsonby, Graham Holter, and the British Guild of Beer Writers (yes, all of you). But above all, my partner Leeanne, a reluctant beer expert, and my son Arlo, who I look forward to sharing a beer with one day (probably around 2025).

picture credits

The photographs in this book are used with the permission of the copyright holders stated below. Images are listed by page number. Photographs of bottles and publicity materials are not listed here. They were primarily obtained from, and are used with the permission of, the breweries who produced them. All other illustrations and pictures are © Quintet Publishing Limited. While every effort has been made to credit contributors, Quintet would like to apologize should there have been any omissions or errors, and would be pleased to make the appropriate correction for future editions of this book.

Key: a = above; b = below; c = center; l = left; r = right

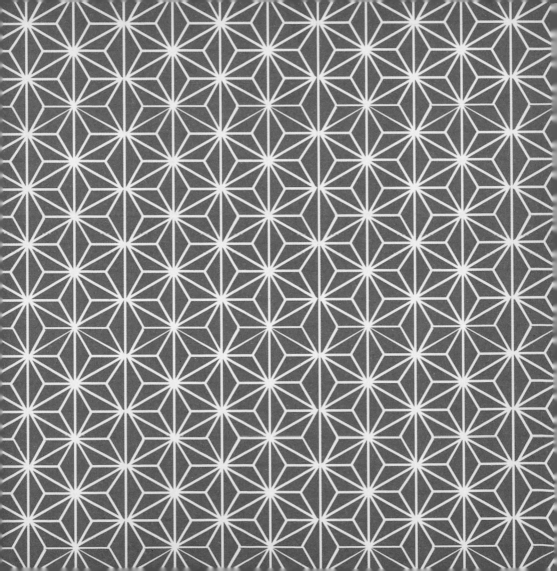